The Tragedy of the European Union

Also by George Soros

Financial Turmoil in the United States and Europe: Essays

The Soros Lectures at the Central European University

The Crash of 2008 and What It Means: The New Paradigm for Financial Markets

The New Paradigm for Financial Markets: The Credit Crisis and What It Means

The Age of Fallibility: Consequences of the War on Terror

Open Society: Reforming Global Capitalism

The Crisis of Global Capitalism: Open Society Endangered

THE TRAGEDY OF THE EUROPEAN UNION

Disintegration or Revival?

GEORGE SOROS

WITH GREGOR PETER SCHMITZ

PublicAffairs NEW YORK

Published in the United States by PublicAffairs™,
a Member of the Perseus Books Group

Printed in the United States of America.

PublicAffairs books are available at special discounts for bulk purchases in the US by corporations, institutions, and other organizations. For more information, please contact the Special Markets Department at the Perseus Books Group, 2300 Chestnut Street, Suite 200, Philadelphia, PA 19103, call (800) 810-4145, ext. 5000, or e-mail special.markets@perseusbooks.com.

BOOK DESIGN BY JENNY DOSSIN

Library of Congress Cataloging-in-Publication Data
Soros, George.
The tragedy of the european union: disintegration or revival? / George Soros with Gregor Peter Schmitz.
pages cm
ISBN 978-1-61039-421-5 (hardcover)—ISBN 978-1-61039-422-2 (ebook)
1. European Union countries—Economic policy. 2. European Union countries—Economic conditions. 3. European Union countries—Politics and government. 4. European Union.
I. Schmitz, Gregor Peter. II. Title.
HC240.S654 2014
337.1'42—dc23
2013049858

FIRST EDITION

1 3 5 7 9 10 8 6 4 2

For Tamiko,

without whom this book would not have been possible.

Contents

Preface by Anatole Kaletsky ix

Introduction by Gregor Peter Schmitz xv

Part 1: Summer 2013

First Interview: History 3

Second Interview: Tragedy 25

Third Interview: Markets 55

Part 2: December 2013

Fourth Interview: Future 93

Appendix: Fallibility, Reflexivity, and the Human Uncertainty Principle 127

Preface

Is it too late to save the European Union? In January 1999, when the euro was created, the single currency project looked like the most decisive step toward Europe's "ever closer union," a process that began with the Treaty of Rome in the aftermath of the Second World War. The euro was supposed to create a unified continental economy that would rival the United States in its economic dynamism and financial stability. It was designed to eradicate the economic divergences that contributed to what Winston Churchill described as Europe's "Thirty-Year Civil War" from 1914 to 1945. And it was supposed to make the EU an even more inspiring model, at the point in history when the Soviet empire was collapsing and the time seemed ripe for new geopolitical arrangements based on mutual economic benefit and democratic cooperation, instead of coercion by imperial powers.

Fifteen years later, it is obvious that this project has gone badly wrong. Xenophobic and neo-fascist movements have gained unprecedented support in the run up to the 2014 European elections. Britain is planning an EU exit referendum. And all over Europe national interests are perceived to be in conflict as governments respond to anti-EU sentiment among their voters. This reversal of European integration is clearly linked to the euro and the global financial crisis. But what exactly went wrong and can it be put right?

If anyone can offer an authoritative answer, it is George Soros. *The Tragedy of the European Union* is deftly organized in a series of in-depth interviews conducted over several months in 2013 by Gregor Peter Schmitz, Europe Correspondent for *Der Spiegel*, one of Europe's leading newsmagazines. Soros's insights, not just on Europe but also on global economic politics and financial markets, are uniquely valuable for three mutually reinforcing reasons: Firstly, because the disintegration of once-great nations and empires is often triggered by financial crises. And nobody understands crises better than Soros. As the world's pre-eminent currency speculator, Soros has shown repeatedly that he understands the interaction of markets and politics better than the people who run finance ministries and central banks. Bolstered by Schmitz's introduction, which astutely frames the major themes and offers context, the interviews in this book present Soros's insights—mainly about Europe, but also about the US, China, the Middle East, and elsewhere—with unprecedented clarity by focusing on specific personal experiences and historical events. Because of his astonishing investment record, his views on finance and economics are always in demand around the world.

But there are two other reasons why Soros's comments in this book could have a greater effect than usual, especially on European policy debates. While Soros has achieved fame as the world's most successful financial speculator, if he is remembered by history it will not be just for making his $20 billion fortune, but for spending it. By creating his Open

Society foundations, Soros helped to tear down the Iron Curtain, demolish the Berlin Wall, and overthrow the communist dictatorships of Eastern Europe and the Soviet Union. Because of his decades of direct engagement in both politics and finance, he brings a personal insight to his analysis that few other commentators, or even politicians, can match.

Soros explains that his faith in the EU goal of "ever-closer union" was inspired by his father, who insisted, even in the midst of the Nazi holocaust, that they should bear no personal grudge against the German people as a whole. Unlike the British euro-sceptics or German conservative economists, who always believed that the single currency was doomed to failure, Soros expected the euro to succeed. For him, the euro crisis was not an inevitable consequence of over-ambitious integration, but a result of avoidable blunders and misunderstandings in politics, economics, and finance.

This emphasis on flawed understanding points to a third feature of Soros's thinking that makes his analysis unique. Soros presents both the euro crisis and the financial collapse related to Lehman Brothers as classic examples of "reflexivity"—a process by which flawed economic or political theories become so powerful that they alter the social realities they are supposed to describe. This interference between perceptions and realities creates waves of instability in markets and political systems that few economists or politicians properly understand. Soros attributes his financial success mainly to focusing on reflexivity, and he uses this concept to diagnose the flaws of the euro project as well as to explain the US banking collapse.

In both cases, a misguided economic theory—the excessive

faith in the self-regulating financial markets that Soros calls market fundamentalism—inspired flawed institutional structures. In Europe, the key institutional flaw was the Maastricht Treaty; in the US it was the excessive reliance on badly designed synthetic financial instruments like collateralized debt obligations and credit default swaps. The false economic theories embodied in these structures changed economic and financial conditions, setting up boom-bust cycles of initial over-performance and over-confidence, followed by self-reinforcing collapse. Because reflexivity is so central to Soros's perspective, this book includes an article from the latest issue of the *Journal of Economic Methodology* in which Soros offers the most detailed and definitive account of his conceptual framework and its implications for economics, politics, and the philosophy of science. Comments from excerpts on Soros's theory can be found in the Winter 2014 issue of *JEM* at www.tandfonline.com/action/aboutThisJournal?journalCode=rjec20.

Nowhere have the reflexive misunderstandings of politicians and financial markets been more widespread and damaging than in Germany. Soros shows with detailed examples why Chancellor Angela Merkel's approach to the euro is widening the divergences between creditor and debtor nations, leaving the subservient debtors resentful and disempowered. As a result, the European ideal of a voluntary community of open societies, linked by mutual economic interests, is beginning to resemble an old-fashioned empire ruled by a domineering German hegemon.

While hegemonic oppression is certainly not the intention either of Germany or the European leadership, the fact is that misguided responses to the euro crisis have turned the EU into a foreign oppressor in the eyes of many of its citizens—and not only in the peripheral states. Even in Britain, the euro crisis has intensified opposition to the entire European project and strengthened demands for total withdrawal from the EU. Many of the arguments Soros presents here could prove very influential both in the upcoming European Parliamentary elections, and in Britain's planned referendum on EU membership, since the evident failure of Europe's most important project is having a profound effect on British views. Soros argues that Britain currently enjoys the best available position, being part of the European Union but not part of the euro. Changing it would be detrimental both for Britain and for Europe as a whole. For Britain, EU withdrawal would undermine London's position as Europe's financial center and threaten foreign investment directed at the European single market. The European Union, in turn, would be diminished by Britain's departure. Britain would cease to play its historic role of maintaining a balance between hostile blocks on the continent. Its departure would powerfully reinforce a process of economic and political disintegration that is already under way.

Yet a British vote to withdraw will become increasingly likely if the eurozone becomes a region of permanent economic stagnation and political alienation. Such an outcome seems almost inevitable to Soros if Germany maintains its present policy of preserving the euro by always offering the smallest possible concessions at the last possible moment.

This is what Soros calls Europe's recurring nightmare. But a nightmare is a horror from which we can wake up. To awaken

Europe Soros proposed a revolutionary notion: that Germany should "lead or leave the euro." Either Germany should lead Europe toward some form of mutual debt and bank guarantees, or it should leave the euro and allow other countries to solve the currency's systemic problems on their own, which according to Soros they would be quite capable of doing. A euro without Germany may sound like a shocking concept, but Soros spells out in detail how a "southern euro," probably led by France, could become a viable currency.

Following the German elections Soros ceased to advocate that Germany should "lead or leave the euro." The German electorate has decisively rejected the idea by keeping the party advocating it below the threshold of parliamentary representation; and no debtor country can afford to advocate it because it would be immediately punished both by the markets and by the European authorities.

For Soros, such a euro break-up was never an optimal solution. Far better would be for Germany to become a "benign hegemon," accepting its responsibility to support the reconstruction of peripheral Europe, as the US supported post-war German reconstruction with the Marshall Plan. Perhaps this could even happen, now that Angela Merkel can contemplate her place in history, instead of her next election campaign. Let us hope Mrs. Merkel reads this book.

Anatole Kaletsky
Chairman of the Institute for New Economic Thinking
and author of *Capitalism 4.0*

Introduction

It may have been her proudest moment, her first undisputed election victory after two previous nail-biters. It was September 22, 2013, and Angela Merkel was standing on the stage at the Konrad Adenauer House in Berlin. The pollsters had predicted a clear victory for Merkel and her Christian Democratic Union (CDU), together with its sister party, the Bavarian Christian Social Union (CSU), and even an absolute majority seemed within reach. Merkel's supporters were jumping up from their seats, and as "*Tage wie diese*" (Days Like These) by the German punk band Die Toten Hosen boomed from the loudspeakers, CDU-CSU parliamentary floor leader Volker Kauder grabbed a microphone and began singing along. CDU secretary general Hermann Gröhe seemed on the verge of waving a small German flag that someone on the stage had handed him. But not on Merkel's watch. Shaking her head in disapproval, she took the flag from his hand and removed it from the stage.

The symbolism was unmistakable. Even in her greatest moment of triumph, the chancellor was being careful not to indulge in German nationalism. After all, the rest of Europe, which had characterized Germany's parliamentary election as a "European election," was watching. Merkel was determined not to allow her victory to be seen as an exuberant display of national pride by people in Europe's crisis-stricken countries, such as Spain, Italy, and Greece. But her intervention was to no avail. The next day, the headline "Merkel, Merkel Über Alles" appeared on the front page of the Spanish daily newspaper *El Mundo*, and the Greek newspaper *Ta Nea* ran the headline: "Europe Is Becoming Merkel-Land."

How could it have come to this? Why is a country that rejects a leadership role in Europe once again being viewed by many as a ruthless hegemon, even a dominant occupying power? Why do protesters wave swastika flags when Merkel visits the Greek capital, Athens? How could the "German question" return with such vehemence, at a time when Germany is in fact one of the most important lenders to the crisis-ridden countries in the European Union (EU)? In his book *Ein Europa, das es nicht gibt* (*A Europe That Doesn't Exist*), University of Bonn professor and historian Dominik Geppert writes: "Some of the political catchphrases of the July crisis after 1914—'encirclement,' 'blank check,' 'flight to the front' and 'a leap into the dark'—feel unexpectedly topical in 2013." Former foreign minister Joschka Fischer apparently holds a similar view. In a piece for the *Süddeutsche Zeitung* in June 2012, he wrote darkly: "In the 20th century, Germany destroyed itself and the European order twice in wars that involved crimes and genocide, in its efforts to subjugate the continent. It would be a tragedy and an irony alike if, at the beginning of the 21st century, a unified Germany were to ruin the European order once again, this time peacefully and with the best of intentions."

These are confusing and even alarming questions, especially when embellished with scenes from the 2013 parliamentary election, in which the newly established Alternative für Deutschland (Alternative for Germany) party held "euro burnings" in front of the Brandenburg Gate in Berlin to draw attention to the fact that Germany is now experiencing the greatest destruction of money since the hyperinflation of 1923. The party's leader, Bernd Lucke, provided "yet another allusion to those times of democracy in crisis," as the *Frankfurter Allgemeine Zeitung* wrote, when he likened an alleged attack on him during a campaign speech to the actions of "gangs of thugs in the Weimar Republic."

Today's times of crisis prevail in a Europe in which euroskeptics and anti-European parties from Greece, Spain, Great Britain, Belgium, France, and Germany are predicted to capture a total of 30 percent of the vote in elections to the European Parliament in May 2014. French president François Hollande warned: "A majority of the European Parliament could consist of anti-Europeans. This presents a true risk of paralysis."

. . .

This book is about Germany and the crisis, including a crisis within its political leadership. But it is also a book about Europe and the weaknesses of its institutions and their future. In a European Union premised on the founding concept of its nation-states progressively moving toward a federation of states, these two poles—the German crisis and the European malaise—are inseparable. "The Treaties of Rome, and later the Maastricht Treaty, expressly affirmed the goal of an 'ever-closer' union. Walter Hallstein, the first and, thus far, only German president of the European Commission [Commission of the European Economic Community], said that the nation state is 'not the unchanged measure of all things political.' From this point of view, it was not a question of salvaging the nation states but of abolishing them. The goal was a United States of Europe as a European federal state," writes historian Dominik Geppert.

In other words, the predominant and uniting ambition was that it would come to pass that important political decisions would no longer be made in Berlin, Paris, and London, but at the European level. This ambition was long the established standpoint in Germany. When top German politicians spoke with George Soros in the 1990s, they assured him that there was no longer a German but only a European foreign policy. And during the years of the euro introduction, then-chancellor Helmut Kohl's declared motto was that a united Germany was only conceivable within a united Europe.

But that consensus has since been shattered. Privately, Merkel, as her biographer Stefan Kornelius fears, has long abandoned the collective model. In her view, the nation-states are responsible for their own plight and should resolve their own problems. In the 2013 election campaign, Merkel was no longer invoking the concept of "more Europe," as the overwhelming majority of her predecessors had done, but instead proposed that powers could be returned to the nation-states—which amounted to "less Europe." Brussels political scientist Jan Techau characterized such scenarios as a "breach of taboo in German foreign policy." It seems that Merkel simply no longer believes in the creative power of European institutions, especially the European Commission, and would rather content herself with bilateral problem-solving approaches, in which Germany sets the tone. So, can we expect to be confronted with Berlin's desire for a "German Europe"? Will close political unity be replaced by the "tragedy of the European Union," as American Nobel laureate Paul Krugman predicts?

Only a few years ago, the project of European unification and the common currency, the euro, was on a roll. In his well-received 2004 book, *The European Dream*, political scientist Jeremy Rifkin explained why Europe—and not the United States—was the world's role model, as did Mark Leonard, the co-founder and director of the European Council on Foreign Relations, in his 2005 book, *Why Europe Will Run the 21st Century*. Such ideas seemed by no means presumptuous at the time. The project of European unification was not just responsible for the longest period of peace on the continent since the sixteenth century. It had also shaped a multinational generation, which, thanks to uncomplicated border crossings and a uniform currency, was living together in greater harmony than any generation before it. In the distant future, historians were to look back on an era in which 7 percent of the world's population was responsible for 32 percent of global trade and 50 percent of global social benefits.

There seemed to be no end in sight to the boom. The word *Europe* was closely linked to economic progress, be it in the form of low telephone rates, subsidies for Sicily, or impoverished parts of Portugal (and, as we sometimes forget, for structurally weak German regions), new industrial construction in Ireland and Spain, or more generally, joining the euro, which promised an additional economic boost. Harvard political scientist Joseph Nye recognized that the EU expansion policy was a global export success, especially compared with the nation-building disaster by the United States in Iraq and Afghanistan. And political scientist Ulrike Guérot even called Europe the "true modern world" when compared with the United States, because its expansion had taken place voluntarily.

During this time, the euro was being praised about as euphorically as the federation. Immediately before the euro crisis erupted, the European Commission was still rejoicing over how well the new currency had developed ten years after its introduction. In many places, the euro was being exuberantly touted as a success story. And Germany? After difficult years of crisis, it was the world's top exporting nation once again. And as the economic engine of Europe, Germany also felt like the heart of the continent—a country no one had to be afraid of.

Did this hubris inevitably lead to tragedy? Today, in the fifth year of the crisis, the European dream feels like a nightmare from which the continent has yet to awaken. In Spain and Greece, for example, almost every other young person is out of work, and people there will have to adapt to decades of stagnation. In his new book, *Das deutsche Europa* (*A German Europe*), sociologist Ulrich Beck warns that the very foundations of the welfare state are at risk, and that this could lead to the emergence of a new European lower class.

. . .

In the following conversations with George Soros, four key questions are addressed that Europe, in light of this epochal crisis, can no longer ignore if it hopes to become a "united federation" made up of politically and economically equal partners, and if it hopes to act as a global player:

1. Does the current European Union still live up to the ideals on which it was founded?

   It remains to be seen whether the community will remember its unique and historic original idea—the realization that on a belligerent continent lasting peace is only possible through cooperation. Can this idea still hold the continent together in times of economic crisis? Can it have a similarly uniting effect at the European level as the American motto "We, the people"? Or does Europe threaten to relapse into the kind of national egoism that once divided the continent?

2. What has caused the euro crisis, and what can we learn from the mistakes that have been made?

   The analysis of mistakes that led to the crisis always sounds surprisingly simple: government failure and waste in the crisis-ridden countries. But is it really that simple? The euro crisis wasn't just based on government borrowing excesses such as those in Greece, but also on the structural defects of a monetary union expected to function without a political union, and in which the countries with large trade surpluses (Germany, for instance) and those with large deficits were united. Only when the European players recognize this fact can they come to an agreement on the best way out of the crisis.

3. What is the current relationship between politics and the market?

   Is Europe merely a pawn of global financial investors, or do politicians still have some influence over the markets? Do they even understand the markets? Or do they use criticism of speculators as an excuse to draw attention away from the structural weaknesses of the system they designed and now control? And could speculation have been curbed earlier if reactions to the first symptoms of the crisis had been more unanimous, such as in the form of collective liability for public debts in individual EU member states?

4. In which direction is the European Union headed?
   Many leading politicians in Europe have long placed their faith in a policy of small steps, driven by acute crises. But is that enough, or does Europe need a so-called Philadelphia moment, that is, the epochal step toward a true political union, like the one the first colonies in the United States took a few years after their declaration of independence, with the ratification of their draft constitution? And what steps would have to follow such a breakthrough? A social union, a union based on joint liabilities, and perhaps even a common European citizenship?

In March 2010, an opinion piece on European crisis management called "Euro Trashed" appeared in the *New York Times*. And during the 2012 American presidential election campaign, the *Wall Street Journal* decreed that any candidate for the White House must, above all, make one thing clear: that the United States is not turning into Europe, an outdated, cowardly, conservative continent that also happens to be deeply in debt. The two pieces reflect America's reactions to Europe, ranging from schadenfreude to true concern. But largely missing in this epochal crisis are intermediaries: between the United States and Europe; more important, among the states within Europe; and, most important, between Germany and the rest of Europe.

Such an intermediary must remind all parties involved that the monetary union was also designed as a political project, which helps to explain some of its structural weaknesses. An intermediary must also explain why the European Union isn't merely the framework for a currency union but is in fact far more: a "confirmation that Europe still plays a role in the world," as former British prime minister Tony Blair put it. And this intermediary must also come up with a viable trade-off between the circumstance that on the one hand, Germany cannot in fact keep the union together on its own and, on the other hand, it is by no means a "victim of the euro," as it likes to portray itself (on the contrary, Germany has benefited considerably from European unification and the establishment of the eurozone). Finally, this intermediary must explain to Germany that it bears a responsibility, not only for historic reasons but also because the poorly conceived monetary union was largely a German project.

But such intermediaries are absent, partly because borders continue to exist in Europe, in defiance of all open barriers, and because a "public space," of the sort German sociologist Jürgen Habermas calls for, has not developed yet, not in the media or in politics, not in the culture of remembrance or within the country's key institutions. When new entities take shape, such as the European Stability Mechanism (ESM), or when existing entities such as the European Central Bank

(ECB) take on an increasingly important role, the key posts in these organizations are not filled through elections but through relatively nontransparent agreements among the member states.

In the euro crisis, there is an unmistakable trend toward renationalization among political leaders. National elections and the media still determine the European rhythm. Most politicians wouldn't think of placing Europe's interests above their national interests, says Ulrich Beck. The sensation caused by a 2001 speech by Polish foreign minister Radosław Sikorski is telling. He could hardly believe what he was saying, Sikorski told his audience in Berlin, but he feared German power less than he was beginning to fear German inactivity. Germany, he noted, should no longer allow itself to be paralyzed by its historic culpability—whereas it threatened to become culpable once again if it did not live up to its responsibility for Europe.

Although Sikorski's clear words had a broad impact, when German politicians discuss issues related to the euro, they tend to sink into "sanitized Lego-language," as British historian Timothy Garton Ash describes it. They are "snapping together prefabricated phrases made of hollow plastic. Most German politicians are more likely to fly unaided to the moon than they are to coin a striking phrase," he writes in the *New York Review of Books*. This leads to a paradox, according to Ash: "while German power has grown, its political class has shrunk." Similar tendencies are recognizable in other member states, where "government failure" often goes hand in hand with the failure of the political leadership.

And yet communication should be more important than

ever. One should no longer see Europe as a question of war and peace. However, European politicians should finally tell their citizens how they intend to cope with the challenges described: the difficult balancing of national interests and common interests, the temptations of national statehood, the role of the markets, and the uncertain future of the union.

Europe needs intermediaries and it needs translators. There is almost no one as qualified to serve in these roles as George Soros, one of the richest men in the world, with a fortune of roughly $20 billion in estimated assets. But Soros has also been a generous philanthropist for decades. Through his Open Society Foundations, he has spent billions to promote democracy and open societies around the world, especially in Eastern Europe.

Soros is familiar with open societies, and with their enemies. As a fourteen-year-old Jewish boy, he had to go into hiding in Budapest when the Nazis invaded Hungary in 1944. There were several times when his life seemed all but lost, and yet his father taught him not to hold any grudges against the Germans, but rather to hold up the hope of European unity.

Many people see Soros as the prototype of the American investor. He immigrated to New York City with a handful of dollars in his pocket in 1956. There, he founded the famous Quantum Fund, among the world's first hedge funds, with which he successfully speculated against the British pound or the Japanese yen and was involved in many spectacular business deals. For many years, he was a "professional Monopoly player," as he puts it. But in his heart, Soros has remained a passionate European, and he believes that throughout the history of mankind, European unity has been the closest thing to an open society. Nevertheless, if the euro crisis escalates, the European Union could face dark times once again, not unlike those Soros experienced himself, first under the Nazis and later in a Communist dictatorship.

When it comes to liberating Europe from the euro crisis, Soros bases his arguments on the lessons of history. He argues that just as he had to learn to react to unusual circumstances by taking unusual measures while living in the underground in Budapest, European politicians must now react in the same way. "There are exceptional times during which the normal rules don't apply. But when the rules are wrong, they must be changed or broken," says Soros, referring to his experiences during the Nazi occupation. Soros argues that it is simply wrong and misguided to stubbornly cling to rules that were once agreed to for the monetary union, if these rules have proven to be inadequate. He also learned something else, he says: to react quickly, and to confront dangers and negative developments head on, no matter how unpleasant this may be. His words are a direct attack on the wait-and-see strategy Angela Merkel is now pursuing in the euro crisis.

This is unusual advice from an unusual human being, someone who has blown up systems and tried to save systems; who has been a ruthless speculator and a generous philanthropist; who was perhaps more successful as a speculator than any investor before him and yet chooses to call himself a "failed philosopher"; and aspires to comparison with such great men as John Maynard Keynes and Albert Einstein, and yet makes a quiet and almost shy impression.

Not surprisingly, Soros has many critics, and their reservations about him are considerable. As a Washington correspondent for *Der Spiegel*, I conducted these interviews with Soros over several months last year to which reactions have been overwhelmingly vehement. "That scoundrel Soros is only thinking of his own interests," one reader wrote. Another suggested that Soros should make his personal assets available to the eurozone's crisis-ridden countries, so that at least the profits he had gained by "underhanded means" would be doing some good. But the most frequent complaint is a question: Why does *Der Spiegel* offer a forum to someone who has almost brought down the global financial system several times, so that he can express his thoughts on the global financial system?

"Who is more qualified to reform the system than someone who was successful within that system?" Soros asks in response to such criticism. Using the classic meaning of the Latin word *specula* (place of observation), Soros sees a "speculator" as someone who, to gain a better perspective, is able to point out deficiencies and weaknesses (even if he occasionally uses them for his own purposes). However, he is not trying to defend speculators across the board. Instead, Soros recognizes that markets often create their own reality and, through their own hysterical overreactions, for example, can easily accelerate and even escalate crises. For this reason, he advocates strict regulation of particularly risky financial instruments, such as credit default swaps (CDS). But one issue is particularly important to him: By branding speculators as the sole catalysts for the euro crisis, European politicians have deflected attention away from the fundamental problem of the monetary union. This is where his analysis coincides with that of many economists, namely, that as long as these structural problems of the monetary union have not been resolved and the crisis-ridden countries are not given a real chance to reestablish their competitiveness, the crisis will not end.

Soros never speculated against the euro during the crisis, even though such critics as Paul Krugman have repeatedly accused him of doing just that. For this reason, there was no sense of concern over private interests in the conversations for this book but rather a deep inner drive. For instance, when asked why, after his third wedding, he is not enjoying his retirement but instead continues to be involved in the European cause, Soros replied: "It might sound crazy, but my idea of a fulfilling life is to be able to influence history. And I'll be a happy man if I can convince the German public—or, in a broader sense, the European public—that it must save the euro and the European Union if it hopes to save itself."

. . .

When the opportunity arose to talk to George Soros about Europe—and to address the four key questions with him—*Der Spiegel* and I did not hesitate. The result is a compendium on the historic foundations of the European Union, which are now more important than ever. It also consists of reflections on Germany's difficult role and an exchange of ideas about the role played by the markets, whose mechanisms Soros knows more than anyone else, but which he believes could be controlled politically if politicians had the courage to enact more prudent legislation. Most of all, these are conversations about the impending transformation of a union of equal nations into an unequal compulsory union of borrowers and creditors, one that threatens to divide the continent once again and undermines the idea of this historically unprecedented union.

If this division ultimately led to the collapse of the union, it would not only be a "German crime against Europe," as Italian journalist Eugenio Scalfari warns, but a crime against Germany's future. As much as Berlin likes to see itself as a "winner in the crisis" today, it is just as clear that Germany, as the greatest beneficiary of a stable eurozone, also stands to lose the most from its breakup, especially as its apparent strength has feet of clay. "Germany could soon be forced to benefit from a European transfer union," warns influential US economist Barry Eichengreen in the Swiss newspaper *Finanz und Wirtschaft*, citing demographic problems, education deficits, and an investment bottleneck.

In other words, the decision to resignedly turn away from the European unification process cannot be the right one for Germany, either, despite its proven usefulness to Merkel at the polls. Instead, it is a question of the chancellor, often dubbed the "world's most powerful woman," finally becoming a European architect in her next term, instead of constantly behaving as Europe's crisis manager, as *Süddeutsche Zeitung* writes.

We hope this book will encourage its readers to bet on Europe. George Soros, my partner in conversation, and I are convinced that a strong commitment to the European Union and to preserving the currency unit is by no means a risky game of chance. Instead, it is a profitable investment in the future of Europe—as well as in the future of Germany, which cannot remain on the winning side and continue to thrive economically while Europe loses its unity and threatens to break apart. Everything else is a myth. And if politicians in Berlin believe that they have already averted an impending European tragedy with their policies to date, their assessment is nothing but a tragic mistake.

Gregor Peter Schmitz
Europe Correspondent, *Der Spiegel*

PART 1
Summer 2013

First Interview: History

Gregor Peter Schmitz: This book deals with the problematic present and the difficult future of the European Union (EU). That union, though, cannot be properly understood without a look at its historical roots—the determination to create peace in war-torn Europe. You became famous as the archetypical "American investor," with an estimated fortune of more than $23 billion, but you remember that dark European past better than most, having grown up in a Jewish family in Hungary in the 1930s. At that time Europe was not a friendly environment for people like you.

George Soros: There was anti-Semitism in Hungary in the 1930s, but that was nothing compared to what came afterward.

Schmitz: Your father changed your family name from Schwartz to Soros to make it sound less Jewish. Did your family try to shed its heritage?

Soros: That was in 1936, which was when I started going to elementary school. It was an attempt to deemphasize our Jewish origin. We were not a religious family. I was brought up in a very liberal atmosphere. My father even contemplated changing our religion because it was a purely formal issue for us, but in the end he decided against it. He felt it would be hypocritical, as we did not believe in religion. But changing the name, making it into a Hungarian name, we felt good about that. Anti-Semitism gave my mother ulcers, but it did not bother me very much. But we were still Jewish, of course, so when I went to gymnasium in 1940, I was put in a Jewish class, and in 1943 I had my bar mitzvah.

SCHMITZ: This topic took on a whole new meaning when the Nazis invaded Hungary in 1944. Did you fear for your life then?

SOROS: Not particularly. We were under the impression the occupation would be short-lived, a few weeks or so. After all, the Nazis were in retreat everywhere and the war seemed to be coming to an end.

SCHMITZ: Instead, the Nazis stayed for twelve months and killed roughly 400,000 Jews in Budapest.

SOROS: Actually, Jews were deported mainly from the Hungarian provinces to be killed at Auschwitz. The Jewish population of Budapest fared somewhat better, largely because of the efforts of various diplomats, of whom Sweden's Raoul Wallenberg became the most famous, to provide some protection. But, eventually, many thousands of Jews were deported from Budapest, too, and the others were put in the ghetto. During the last days of the war, a lot of them were executed by the Hungarian Arrow Cross. One day I passed two bodies hanging from a lamppost in the middle of Budapest. Affixed to one was a sign reading: "This is what happens to a Jew who hides."

Schmitz: That scared you?

Soros: Of course, yet I felt relatively safe because we were prepared. My father had foreseen what was coming and had arranged false identities for us. He saved not only the family, but also a number of other people.

Schmitz: How did your father organize the false papers?

Soros: He found a peacetime forger, somebody who made a living by preparing forged documents. My father became that man's biggest customer. Most important, the concierge of a building my father managed was grateful for the way my father had treated him over the years and offered his help. He gave us the papers of his entire family, which meant we then had a complete set of documents. My father used it quite extensively. We then forged individual documents for imaginary members of that family, and there were several people whose dates of birth differed from the others only by a few months. Therefore, there were certain pairs of people who could never be together because they were brothers or sisters with only three months between them—and that doesn't look very correct. So, it was quite a complicated thing—who could be together with whom.

Schmitz: Do you remember a situation when you were in

hiding in which you thought, "It's all over. We're going to be found out"?

SOROS: Never, although there were moments of danger, to be sure. Once I was recognized by a schoolmate in Budapest and had to move to a different location. The very first weekend when I was on my own, separate from my family and living with a false identity, I went for a walk, and without realizing it, I left the perimeter of Budapest. There was a police patrol asking for identification and this was my first experience using false papers. So, yes, I was pretty scared. But while I was aware of the dangers, I was also confident that I would survive. Of course, had I been caught, I would have perished.

SCHMITZ: "I would have perished." That sounds so matter of fact. One almost gets the impression that that year in the underground was one big adventure for you.

SOROS: It was. In fact, 1944 was the formative experience of my life. The important and paradoxical point is that it was the happiest year of my life. This is a strange, almost offensive thing to say because of course it was a horrible and tragic time for most people. But, I was fourteen years old. I had a father I adored, who was in command of the situation, who knew what to do, and who helped others. We were in mortal danger, but we were on the side of the angels. When you are fourteen years old, you believe that you can't really be hurt, and I was living through the most exciting adventure that one could possibly ask for. I learned the art of survival from a grand master. I loved my father deeply and was extremely happy to be able to spend so much time with him. That experience shaped my behavior for the rest of my life.

SCHMITZ: What did your father teach you during that time?

SOROS: That there are exceptional times during which the normal rules don't apply, and if you abide by those rules, you may perish. He was a lawyer by training but really took this lesson to heart—you have to take your fate into your own hands, and that's what my father did in World War II. He learned that in World War I. He was a prisoner of war in a Siberian camp. There, he organized a breakout of prisoners; they fled across the taiga and lived through the Russian Revolution. That was the formative experience of *his life*, and he told me about it in small installments. We used to meet daily after school in the swimming pool. My father's experience in World War I shaped his actions in World War II, and, of course, my experience under his guidance shaped my subsequent character and behavior, both as an investor and as a human being.

SCHMITZ: How so?

SOROS: Well, primarily, in making me realize that it's better to confront harsh reality than to passively submit to it, and it may be safer to take a risk than to avoid it. We are seeing this in Europe right now, where political leaders tend to downplay the severity of the current crisis and kick problems down the road. I am energized by emergencies. I tend to anticipate the worst, think creatively, and find a better outcome. I learned that from my father. When the Nazis invaded Hungary, my father knew immediately that we had to adopt false identities and disappear, so he started working on it right away. I became "János Kis," as my forged passport said. That is what saved our lives.

Schmitz: You described in your memoirs that other Jewish citizens in Budapest told you at that time: "We are still going to comply with the law because we are law-abiding citizens."

Soros: There was one particular experience that stood out. All Jewish students in Budapest were ordered to work for the Jewish Council. My first job was to deliver notices to a list of people, which turned out to be a list of Jewish lawyers. The notice ordered them to report to the Rabbinical Seminary with clothing, a blanket, and food for twenty-four hours. I took the notices to my father, who told me to deliver the notices, but tell the people that if they report, they will be deported. One lawyer said to me, "I've been a law-abiding citizen all my life, and therefore, I should be safe if I report." And, of course, he wasn't. That incident made a lasting impression on me.

Schmitz: I understand your reaction. Then again, the rule of law is a cornerstone of every functioning society.

Soros: It is. And promoting the rule of law is one of the cornerstones of my philanthropy. But when the rules are wrong, they must be changed or broken. Right now, for example, the European authorities are biding by antiquated treaties and causing a lot of unnecessary suffering.

SCHMITZ: What was your view of Germans at that time?

SOROS: My father drew a very sharp distinction between the Nazi regime and the German people, which meant he did not hold people personally responsible for the regime. Again, in that respect, I had a memorable experience. My father used to spend his days in a café even when he was in hiding, and he was a very outgoing person. He befriended strangers, and one day he actually made friends with a German officer.

SCHMITZ: That was while you were in hiding?

SOROS: Oh, yes. But instead of hiding, my father hung out in public because he considered that safer.

SCHMITZ: Were you with him in the café when he befriended the officer?

SOROS: I was. We used to meet there regularly. This officer, who was a pharmacist in Breslau in civilian life, complained to my father how unhappy he was because of his duties. My father consoled him, saying that he was only carrying out his duties, so he should not feel bad about it as long as he was doing his best to help people rather than to hurt them. It was an ironic situation for a Jew in hiding to be consoling a German officer.

SCHMITZ: Did you understand at that time what your father was doing?

SOROS: Of course. I absorbed his values, not uncritically, because one of his values was to be critical and not to follow instructions slavishly. But this particular episode keeps coming to my mind when I look at my own efforts to persuade Germany to change its policies. I don't want Germans to become objects of hatred in the rest of Europe again.

SCHMITZ: When the war was over, after you had survived, what were your expectations for Europe? Did you even think it was possible that there would ever be lasting peace?

SOROS: It was a period of reconstruction and revival and there was the Marshall Plan. The Marshall Plan led to the European Union because it was not only assisting individual countries; it was setting up mechanisms for cooperation, reopening commerce, and building a European economy. It was probably the most successful example ever of official development assistance. And it showed the benevolent side of America, which held a hegemonic position in Europe similar to the position that Germany holds today. The difference is that the Americans embarked on the Marshall Plan and debt forgiveness, whereas Germany today insists on the full payment of debts without offering any similar plans for Europe's economic revival and political reconstruction.

SCHMITZ: Initially, though, not everyone in the United States was so generous. The Morgenthau plan aimed for the deindustrialization of Germany. Did you sympathize with the desire to keep Germany down after the horrors of the Holocaust?

Soros: No. My father was an Esperantist and a believer in international cooperation. I grew up in that spirit. It was the obvious way to go, and the idea of vengeance or retribution was emotionally alien to us. As a student at the London School of Economics (LSE) in the early 1950s, I pursued that inherited interest and studied past attempts at international cooperation—the League of Nations, customs unions, commodity buffer schemes, John Maynard Keynes, Bretton Woods, and so on.

Schmitz: In 1956, you left Europe to go to New York City. Did you feel you could succeed more easily in the United States?

Soros: When you don't have any money, you worry about it a lot. That was the time of the dollar gap, and I wanted to close my own dollar gap by going to New York. It may sound silly now, but I actually had a five-year plan—very popular in Soviet times. My aim was to go to America and make a fortune of $100,000 and then come back to England and devote myself to philosophy. That was my five-year plan, and I actually exceeded it. I made more than $100,000.

Schmitz: But you stayed on.

Soros: I got caught up in the money-making game and went on to make a fortune. However, the financial markets also turned out to be a great laboratory for putting my philosophical theories to a practical test.

SCHMITZ: So you changed your plan—but you maintained your interest in Europe?

SOROS: Very much so. The European Union is in my view the shining example of an open and free society. That is why the current crisis is so personal to me. I am very concerned about Europe's future and the potential dissolution of its open society. In the run-up to World War I or in the Weimar Republic, people did not think all those terrible things that followed could happen. But I have a particular sensitivity to these matters, because I lived under both Nazi and Soviet occupation. And I would hate to see a repeat of dark times in Europe.

SCHMITZ: When you met with European leaders over the decades, did they share your perspective?

SOROS: In 1989, I spent an extended period in Germany and met with a number of German politicians and public figures, and they unanimously proclaimed that Germany had no independent foreign policy, only a European policy. That was the refrain of all those conversations. Of course, Germany was at that time, along with France, at the forefront of European integration. It was a farsighted vision, that Germany could be reunited only in the context of a united Europe. Helmut Kohl was willing to make considerable sacrifices to achieve reunification. At the same time, President Mitterrand and the French political establishment—and I had a number of conversations with the French political elite at that time—were pretty unanimous in recognizing that France had no chance to remain a world power without being closely associated with Germany, because Germany could expand eastward but France could not expand southward. So it's those two motivations that gave the impetus to a greatly accelerated process of European integration.

SCHMITZ: Helmut Kohl sometimes referred to himself as the direct successor to Adolf Hitler because he was the first chancellor of the reunited Germany.

SOROS: The French were also using Nazi terminology when they spoke of a "Lebensraum."

SCHMITZ: When you spoke to leaders in France, Great Britain, or Germany, how often did that specter of the past come up?

SOROS: That generation of Germans was weighed down by an overwhelming sense of guilt for the atrocities committed by the Hitler regime. That was why Germany wanted to subordinate itself to a European political union in order to escape even the possibility of a repetition. This was the motivating factor in a genuine desire not to dominate. And I think that attitude is still very strong in Germany today. Germany does not want to dominate Europe, but the willingness to make sacrifices has disappeared. At that time, Germany was always willing to give a little more, and take a little less. That is what made the process of integration so successful for a time.

SCHMITZ: Do you remember when that attitude began to change among German politicians?

Soros: The impulse for closer integration culminated with the German reunification and the introduction of the euro. In a way, the euro was the price that François Mitterrand demanded for supporting reunification, so it was a deal between Kohl and Mitterrand, that in exchange for French support, Germany would agree to a common currency.

When both of these goals were achieved, conditions changed. Reunification turned out to be very expensive for Germany, because the economy in the East was barely functioning. Germany became weighed down by very heavy debts and had to tighten its belt. So the generosity that promoted the process of integration disappeared.

Schmitz: What did you think of the euro when it was announced? You said it was the price to pay, but from the perspective of an investor, was the price too high?

Soros: I was a great supporter of the euro, although I recognized, as others did, that it was an incomplete currency. It was a monetary union without a political union. The euro had a central bank, but not a common treasury. I think that was obvious to everyone. But remember that the introduction of the common currency was meant to be a step toward further integration. The process of creating the European Union was an exercise in what Karl Popper called "piecemeal social engineering"—taking a small step, setting a particular target and timetable, then generating public support for that step, knowing full well that it will necessitate further steps. That is how the European Steel and Coal Community was transformed into the European Union step by step.

SCHMITZ: The British historian Timothy Garton Ash wrote in *Foreign Affairs* that the whole process of piecemeal unification in Europe began to fall apart when the euro was introduced because it was so structurally flawed. Would you agree?

SOROS: Only in retrospect. At that time, I regarded it as a step in the right direction. Then the reunification of Germany and the introduction of the euro was followed by a period of digestion. During this period, the financial system of Europe became more integrated into the global financial system. That made it vulnerable to the financial crisis of 2007–2008 that originated in the United States. Because of the globalization of financial markets, that crisis actually caused greater losses for the European financial institutions than for the Americans because the unsound, toxic, and synthetic instruments had found a better market in Europe than in America.

SCHMITZ: When the euro was introduced, what was the perception of your fellow investors in the United States?

SOROS: There were critical voices, but on the whole, the euro managed to establish itself and gain confidence. It seemed to fit into the global integration of financial markets. The financial authorities in Europe did not recognize the most serious, fatal flaw in the euro, and neither did I or my fellow fund managers.

None of us realized that when the individual member countries transferred their right to print money to the European Central Bank (ECB), their government bonds became denominated in a currency that they did not control. They controlled the currency as a group but not individually. That put them in the same position as Third World countries that were borrowing in dollars or in euros. That meant that they ran the risk of default. As long as you can print money, you have no reason to default because you can always service your debt; so the risk of default is absent. But when you are borrowing in a foreign currency, there is that risk, and it was ignored both by the authorities and by the financial markets.

SCHMITZ: Do you recall any conversations with other investors who foresaw that risk at that time?

SOROS: No. The problem did not seem to be of practical significance because the financial authorities made the rules and the rules declared government bonds to be riskless. The European Central Bank accepted the government debt of all the member countries at its discount window on equal terms, and the European banking authorities did not require commercial banks to put aside any of their own equity for the risk involved in holding government bonds. And that created a perverse incentive for commercial banks to invest in government bonds and buy the bonds of the weaker countries that paid higher rates of interest in order to earn a higher profit margin because they could then take those bonds to the ECB and borrow 100 percent against them. The banking authorities considered that a riskless transaction, so the banks could invest an infinite amount. That led the interest rates of the various government bonds to converge. By that time, we were a little suspicious of the extent of the convergence, but we did not dare to speculate against it as long as the European

Central Bank was willing to discount those bonds on equal terms. So we observed the convergence, but we had no reason to believe that it would be reversed.

SCHMITZ: Were you tempted to speculate against the euro?

SOROS: We were more inclined to go with the trend that kept the euro overvalued. Central banks and sovereign wealth funds, which have a much bigger influence on exchange rates than short-term speculators, were accumulating euros. Keep in mind, the creation of the euro greatly reduced the scope for currency speculation because it reduced the number of currencies in which one could trade. That did not turn me against the euro, however, because I considered it to be a very desirable political project, and I thought that I could certainly find other ways of making money.

SCHMITZ: We spoke about the sense of history in Europe. If you look at the current crisis, would a person like Helmut Kohl, who lived through World War II, have handled this crisis differently than Angela Merkel, who lacks that experience?

SOROS: Yes, I think so. Remember, the big break came after the bankruptcy of Lehman Brothers in September 2008, when financial markets were on the verge of a meltdown and the financial authorities had to reassure the markets by saying that they would not allow any other systemically important bank to fail. This happened in October. The finance ministers of the European countries left the International Monetary Fund (IMF) conference in Washington a day early and met in Paris and made this reassuring declaration about protecting all their important banks. But, subsequently, Chancellor Merkel insisted that the guarantee should be given by each country individually, not by the European Union collectively—thereby severely undermining the guarantee. In saying that, she was reading the prevailing German public opinion correctly, because there had been this radical shift in sentiment where Germany no longer wanted to be the deep pocket of Europe and was concerned about the extent of its own debt.

SCHMITZ: Kohl would have handled it differently?

SOROS: Probably he would have used the opportunity to take EU integration a step further by converting the debt of individual countries into eurobonds. That would have avoided the euro crisis. After Merkel's statement that each country had to stand by its own banking system, the panic briefly subsided, but eventually the markets discovered the key flaw in the euro: the real danger that individual governments can default because their debt is not guaranteed by all members of the eurozone. Individual countries were not strong enough to support their banks with huge guarantees. The absence of a credible European bank guarantee was a major contributor to the euro crisis.

SCHMITZ: Was that because Merkel no longer saw the European Union as a matter of war and peace as previous leaders in Germany did?

SOROS: Not necessarily. She has made it clear that the euro is here to stay, that Germany is committed to the euro. At the same time, she has also made it clear that Germany doesn't want to be the deep pocket to sustain the euro and therefore is only willing to do the absolute minimum that is necessary to preserve the euro.

There is an internal contradiction in that position. On the one hand, you have a deeply felt commitment to the euro, but there is also a very strong determination to take on as few liabilities as possible in making the euro work. This internal contradiction is at the root of the euro crisis. It means that the creditor countries, such as Germany, provide support to the weak ones extremely reluctantly and keep it at an absolute minimum. This pushes the heavily indebted countries into a deflationary trap. Cutting the budget at a time of insufficient demand reduces demand even further, because the governments have to impose drastic cuts in public spending instead of providing unemployment benefits and a real safety net. The social safety net—which was the pride of the European Union in the past—doesn't work, just when you need it the most.

SCHMITZ: Are you saying that Germany's leadership runs counter to the whole premise behind the European unification process, which was built on cooperation rather than domination?

SOROS: Yes. And that creates two problems, one political and the other financial. The political problem is that the European Union that was meant to be a voluntary association of equal states has been converted into a relationship between creditors and debtors where, when debtors are unable to pay, the creditors dictate the terms. That gives the creditors much greater influence over the policies of the debtor countries than the debtors have on the policies of the creditor countries.

The financial problem is that Germany, in order to keep its liabilities to a minimum, forces the debtor countries to balance their budgets, which is the wrong policy at a time of insufficient demand, when you should be stimulating the economy.

SCHMITZ: In the past, "more Europe" almost always meant more economic progress, particularly in the poorer countries of the continent, and now it is associated with austerity, cutbacks, high unemployment.

SOROS: Even worse: the prospect is for long-lasting stagnation. That is my main concern and worry. Europe, which is in many ways the most developed part of the world—and the biggest influence on the rest of the world as the cradle of our global civilization—is in a state of economic and political disintegration. Many nations have gone through long periods of stagnation and survived. Latin America suffered a lost decade in the banking crisis of the 1980s. Japan is just now trying to break out of a quarter century of stagnation. But the European Union is not a nation; it is a voluntary and incomplete association of nations that may not survive a long period of stagnation. Moreover, this dismal prospect is portrayed as inevitable, although it could easily be escaped. That is a nightmare, where you are caught up in a situation that seems inescapable and yet all you have to do is wake up.

SCHMITZ: How could you escape it?

SOROS: All you have to do is recognize that the rules that govern the euro are no longer appropriate and need to be changed. During the period of European integration, the rules of the European Union were subject to continuing change and revision and improvement. Instead of that, a patently flawed set of rules has now become immutable because any treaty change has become inconceivable.

SCHMITZ: You mean to say it would be rejected?

SOROS: It's worse than that. Europe's leaders—especially Chancellor Merkel—are not even willing to consider any solutions that don't fit into the existing treaties. If they did, they could build a strong case that could make a treaty change politically possible and even popular.

Having studied the issue very closely, I see two alternatives. Either of which would be preferable to the prevailing state of affairs. One is that Germany would accept its dominant position and the responsibilities and liabilities that go with it, in which case Germany would become a benevolent imperial power in Europe, similar to the United States after World War II. The other alternative is for Germany to leave the euro and thereby allow the rest of Europe, the debtor countries, to take possession of the euro. Since the accumulated debt is denominated in euros, it makes all the difference who remains in charge of the euro. If Germany left, the euro would depreciate. Debtor countries would regain their competitiveness; their debt would diminish in real terms; and, with the ECB under their control, the threat of default would disappear.

SCHMITZ: But wouldn't a eurozone without Germany be seen by investors as weak?

SOROS: Not at all. It would compare favorably with Britain on all recognized measures of strength, debt to gross domestic product (GDP) ratio, growth prospects, and so on. Therefore it should be able to issue bonds at interest rates similar to British gilts.

The creditor countries would incur losses on their claims and investments denominated in euros and encounter stiffer competition at home from other eurozone members. The extent of creditor countries' losses would depend on the extent of the depreciation, giving them an incentive to keep the depreciation within bounds. That should insure that a euro without Germany would be a stable currency.

This would be a big shock for Germany, but it would be a big relief for the other countries. Either alternative would be preferable, even for Germany, than to continue on the current course. But that is not how Germany sees it, and therefore these alternatives cannot even be considered.

SCHMITZ: On what grounds do you say that both alternatives would be preferable even for Germany?

SOROS: The European authorities are forcing all those who find current policies intolerable into anti-European and anti-German attitudes. The rise of anti-European political movements—Beppe Grillo, Marine Le Pen, the UK Independence Party (UKIP), Golden Dawn, you name it—may eventually lead to the breakup of the European Union. I am convinced that is not what Chancellor Merkel or the large majority of Germans want. So it would be important to distinguish between the euro and the European Union and to realize that the euro is a means to an end. And the end is to find a European solution rather than for each country to seek a national solution. We need somehow to recapture the original impulse that led to the creation of the union, the spirit of solidarity and cooperation. Only Germany is in a position to initiate the process.

Schmitz: Is that why you always single out the Germans in your criticism?

Soros: Yes. Germany is by far the strongest power in Europe today, and with this power comes responsibility. Only Germany can end the nightmare that afflicts Europe, because only Germany is in a position to initiate any substantial changes in policy. If any of the debtor countries tried to do so, they would only provoke punishment both from the European authorities and the financial markets. So if I could manage to give a wake-up call to the German public and change public opinion there, I would consider that the crowning achievement of my life. In all other cases I was merely accelerating the tide of history; in this case I would be reversing it.

Second Interview: Tragedy

Gregor Peter Schmitz: Well-known German sociologist Ulrich Beck said that Germany used to be the eager pupil in Europe, and now it acts like a strict schoolmaster. Would you agree?

George Soros: It is an apt description because the Germans want the rest of Europe to learn to be like Germany. But that is impossible. Germany has the best-performing economy in Europe today. But everybody cannot be first at the same time.

To be sure, Germany cannot be blamed for wanting a strong currency and a balanced budget. But it can be blamed for imposing its predilection on other countries that have different needs and preferences—like Procrustes in Greek mythology, who forced other people to lie in his bed and stretched them or cut off their legs to make them fit. The Procrustes bed in which the eurozone has to lie is called austerity and, ultimately, deflation.

Schmitz: From a German perspective, isn't their attitude justified? The country has undergone strict reforms to become competitive again, and it has spent billions of its own dollars to bail out other nations that cheated on the eurozone criteria. Why should they not have to listen to Berlin?

SOROS: There are several reasons why Europeans don't want to listen to advice from Berlin. Let's start with the least important but easiest to understand: Germany's tone, which is sometimes self-righteous and even hypocritical. Look at Germany's own record. Germans accuse other countries of cheating on the euro stability criteria, but they forget that in 2003 Germany was among the first countries to break the eurozone rules. It is a common pattern that people can see the sins and faults of others but forget their own. And now, in the coalition agreement, Germany is raising minimum wages and pensions and permitting earlier retirement, just when it tells other countries to do the opposite. To be sure, raising the minimum wage is the right policy, but a populist rabble-rouser can easily argue that Germany is preaching austerity abroad and doing the opposite at home.

SCHMITZ: But pushing for reforms in other countries can be seen as a modern version of a Marshall Plan. Germany could serve as a role model that could show other nations how to prosper through reform.

SOROS: Now you are going too far. Your reference to the Marshall Plan reminds me of George Orwell's Newspeak. The government does something bad and then justifies it by simply changing the name to "good." The Marshall Plan created growth and promoted postwar reconstruction through a transfer of resources from America that included a generous cancellation of debts. The present European policy creates stagnation and discourages investment by transferring resources back to Germany and demanding repayment of debts on punitive terms.

Even when it comes to structural reforms, presenting Germany as a model is somewhat misleading. Structural reforms worked very well for Germany and have made Germany the most successful country in Europe. But what was successful in Germany before the crisis will not be successful as a prescription for the rest of Europe in the years ahead. That seems very difficult for the Germans to understand, you know, "It worked for us. Why shouldn't it work for you?" But actually it should be quite obvious that it will not work.

SCHMITZ: Why not?

SOROS: Partly because the global economy is now very different from the time when the Schröder government undertook its reforms. Then, the rest of Europe and the world was enjoying a boom and Germany could have an export-led recovery. Now, households, banks, and governments are trying to rebuild their balance sheets worldwide. More important, what worked for one medium-sized export-driven economy such as Germany will not work for a huge economic bloc like the eurozone. Europe as a whole will always depend primarily on internal demand.

SCHMITZ: Still, wouldn't it be better for the other euro countries to try to become more competitive?

SOROS: You're right about that. But even while Germany rightly calls on other countries to try harder, its policy response to the euro crisis makes competitiveness more difficult, or even impossible, to achieve. The fact is that what are now called the "peripheral" countries have accumulated very large debts—and are therefore at a competitive disadvantage. And this disadvantage is becoming even more pronounced through the punitive policies currently in place. The high-risk premiums the so-called peripheral countries have to pay means that they have to spend a few extra percentage points of their GDP every year just to stay even with Germany.

SCHMITZ: Whose fault is that?

SOROS: Germans would say that it is obviously the fault of the debtor countries. But that is because in German the word *Schuld* has a double meaning (both "blame" and "debt"). So it is natural (*selbstverständlich*) to blame the debtor countries for their own misfortunes. But the truth is more complicated.

SCHMITZ: Whom do you blame?

SOROS: The introduction of the euro. Remember the fatal flaw in the euro that neither the authorities nor the markets recognized. By declaring government bonds riskless, the European authorities created a perverse incentive that caused interest rates to converge. And the convergence of interest rates caused divergence in performance. Lower interest rates in the weaker countries allowed them to enjoy a real estate, investment, and consumption boom that left them even weaker when the bubble burst. At the same time, the cost of reunification induced the Schröder government to undertake fiscal and labor market reforms that made Germany even stronger than it had been before. When the financial markets reimposed interest rate differentials, they effectively relegated the weaker countries to the status of heavily indebted Third World countries. That is how they came to be called "periphery" and Germany became the center. The periphery is now at a disadvantage that it will never be able to overcome. And to make matters worse, the weaker countries became saddled in the first decade of the euro's existence with much more debt than a Third World country would ever have been able to accumulate.

SCHMITZ: Why should that be Germany's fault?

SOROS: Because the euro was essentially a Franco-German project. So the excessive *Schuld* of the periphery countries is to a large extent Germany's *Schuld*. Moreover, Germany joined an association of states. In such an association, there has to be a sense of solidarity, not just competition. As I've said, not everybody can be number one. If you want countries to observe mutual obligations, there has to be a quid pro quo of mutual support.

SCHMITZ: So is your criticism of Germany's policy basically on moral grounds?

SOROS: Both on moral and intellectual grounds. Leaving aside the solidarity issue, the German emphasis on competitiveness is intellectually incoherent. Not everybody can achieve a trade surplus, because for every trade surplus, there has to be a deficit. That is simply a matter of arithmetic. So to insist that everybody should have a trade surplus is to insist on suspending the laws of arithmetic. If Germany does insist on this mathematical impossibility, it may end up destroying the European Union.

SCHMITZ: Nevertheless, nearly all economists agree that Europe cannot recover unless the countries in crisis eventually adopt a combination of austerity and reforms.

SOROS: That's not correct at all. What you say may be true about "nearly all" economists within Germany. But outside Germany, nearly all economists believe exactly the opposite: that fiscal austerity is the wrong policy. And I would argue that it is a profound political mistake. In fact, quite a few distinguished economists inside Germany—for example, Peter Bofinger and Dennis Snower—would agree with me. We all recognize the need for structural reforms in individual countries (including more reforms in Germany itself to remove barriers to competition, particularly in services). But most economists outside Germany believe that austerity is preventing growth—and recently the US Treasury pointed out that Germany's trade surplus reflected a weakness of domestic demand that is more destabilizing to the global economy than the policies of Japan or China. So Germans are simply wrong if they think their government leads some kind of consensus of economically responsible nations. At international gatherings such as the IMF or the Organization for Economic Cooperation and Development (OECD), Germany actually has almost no allies—and among the leading economies of the Group of Seven (G7), Germany is literally in a minority of one. Other G7 nations now unanimously recognize that the global economy is in a totally different phase from the one that prevailed when Germany was implementing its reforms and drafting the original rules of the euro.

SCHMITZ: Is it really relevant to go back in history to that point?

SOROS: I think it helps. When the EU agreed on the Maastricht Treaty in 1991, the global economy was in the early stages of a twenty-five-year boom. Then came the crash in 2008. That completely changed the economic and financial conditions. The financial markets actually collapsed, and they had to be put on artificial life support, by substituting the credit of the state for the credit of financial institutions that were temporarily insolvent. The financial authorities embarked on a delicate two-phase maneuver by injecting large amounts of credit in order to bring a financial crisis caused by an excessive growth of credit under control—like when a car is skidding, you have to turn into the direction of the skid and only when you regain control can you turn the wheel back in the direction in which you want to go. The Federal Reserve was successful in carrying out the first phase of this operation and it is only now reaching the point where it is contemplating the second phase. That's making financial markets all around the world very nervous. But the eurozone has made very little progress even in the first phase. That is because of the fatal flaw in the euro that I have been talking about.

When Chancellor Merkel insisted that each country should take care of its own banks, she put additional pressure on the "periphery countries" that were already overextended in what was effectively a foreign currency and forced them into the same pro-cyclical policies that had caused the Great Depression of the 1930s. The rest of the world learned something from that experience, but apparently the German government did not.

SCHMITZ: I know that John Maynard Keynes, the intellectual father of a stimulus-driven economic policy, is one of your heroes. Do you think the Germans ever understood Keynes? After all, the German economy is so export driven that domestic demand was never particularly important to the Germans. Instead, we have always worried about inflation.

SOROS: You are right about Germany's refusal to listen to Keynes. That resistance really goes back to folk memories of runaway inflation: first the traumatic experience of Weimar inflation in the early 1920s and then again in the immediate postwar years, before the creation of the deutsche mark, when the strongest currency in Germany was a pack of Camel cigarettes. So the whole philosophy of the Bundesbank was based on avoiding runaway inflation.

SCHMITZ: There was a survey last year in Germany revealing that Germans are more afraid of inflation than of life-threatening diseases.

SOROS: I am not surprised.

SCHMITZ: Isn't that sentiment understandable? Many Germans associate the rise of Hitler with hyperinflation.

Soros: That may be the accurate reading of German folk memory, but it is an inaccurate reading of history. It is true that hyperinflation wiped out the savings of the middle class after World War I and turned them into a Lumpenproletariat, which was a breeding ground for Nazi sympathies. But let us remember what caused the runaway inflation. It was the excessive war debt imposed on Germany by France and Britain—and the unforgiving determination of the victor nations to collect these debts. One of the tragic ironies of today's euro crisis is that Germany is now making a similar mistake: insisting that all debts should be paid in full and imposing excessively strict austerity that is likely to backfire.

Germans should also recall what actually brought Hitler to power. It was not the Weimar hyperinflation that ended in 1923; it was the terrible unemployment that resulted from the Great Depression of 1929–1932. In 1928, the Nazis gained just 3 percent of the votes in the Reichstag, and in 1929, Erich Ludendorff got just 1.1 percent in the presidential election. It was only in 1930, after America stopped lending Germany money and unemployment jumped from 8 percent to 30 percent, that the Nazis really started gaining votes. When Germany stopped lending money to Greece, Portugal, and Spain after the 2008 crisis, their unemployment rates also jumped to around 30 percent—let us hope we don't see similar political results.

Schmitz: But again: Isn't it sensible and ultimately beneficial to ask nations such as Greece, Spain, or Italy to finally get their budgets and economies in order?

SOROS: Yes in the case of Greece, but the situation in Italy and Spain was and is emphatically different.

SCHMITZ: So you agree that the Greek government falsified its statistics to get into the euro and continued to cheat after that?

SOROS: The Greek government blatantly violated the treaties, but the other debtors generally played by the rules. Indeed, Spain and Ireland used to be held up as paragons of prudent fiscal management—their annual government deficits and their total levels of government debt were both much lower than Germany's as recently as 2009.

SCHMITZ: But even if, as you say, some of the countries that succumbed to the crisis actually abided by the euro treaties, that is now water under the bridge. Are you saying that Germany should now pay for some of the mistakes made in designing the euro by bailing out other countries? That is against European law.

SOROS: You are right about European law. The Maastricht Treaty, which as I said was largely designed by the Bundesbank, contains a clause that expressly prohibits bailouts. And that ban has been reaffirmed by the German Constitutional Court. It is this so called no-bailout clause that has made the current situation so difficult to deal with. But this only proves that the faults revealed by the euro crisis were systemic and rooted in the history of the euro's creation; they were not just a consequence of bad economic policies in the debtor nations.

Schmitz: Are you saying that the Maastricht rules are wrong and should not be enforced?

Soros: Yes, some of the rules need to be changed.

Schmitz: Which specific rules?

Soros: The bailout clause, for one.

Schmitz: What other clauses of the Maastricht Treaty would you change?

Soros: The Maastricht Treaty needs a general overhaul. It was based on a false economic theory, championed mainly by the Bundesbank and the German government. The treaty took it for granted that only government borrowing could produce chronic deficits and destabilize the currency union. That was a serious mistake. Only Greece had a genuine fiscal crisis. In Spain and Ireland, the crisis was caused by housing booms and banking excesses. Italy was a special case. It was weighed down by excessive government debts inherited from the pre-euro period, which became unsustainable when markets imposed heavy risk premiums. Germany refuses to accept this, but it would be well advised to remember its own history.

Schmitz: What part of its history?

Soros: Germany has benefited from debt write-downs three times in its history. The first two happened after World War I. The Dawes Plan of 1924 sought to stagger Germany's reparations payments. The Young Plan of 1929 reduced the sum that Germany owed in reparations and gave the country much more time to pay. These debt-forgiveness plans tried to reverse the mistakes made by the victorious Allies in the Versailles Treaty. After World War I, the French and other victorious powers created economic conditions that helped fascism take root in Germany; tragically, the Germans are doing the same in Greece today, as we see from the rise of the neo-fascist movement Golden Dawn. The French insistence on payment of Germany's post-Versailles obligations was clearly a huge mistake. Keynes was the first to point it out in his *The Economic Consequences of the Peace*, published in 1919.

The third and biggest debt write-down happened after World War II. The Americans and British were careful not to repeat the mistake of the previous generation and instead of seeking reparations, decided to forgive most of Germany's debts. That came in 1953, when the allies canceled half of Germany's debts and rescheduled the rest for very long periods (which is more or less what Greece now needs Germany to do). Without this generosity from the United States and Britain, the German economic miracle would have been completely impossible.

SCHMITZ: Do German politicians listen to you?

SOROS: Not at all, and that is very sad. I remember the days when Chancellor Helmut Kohl showed real leadership. He went to French president François Mitterrand and effectively said to him: Let's create a stronger Europe in which the reunified Germany can be fully embedded. This gave a tremendous push to integration. But the present generation of political leaders in Berlin abandoned the historical perspective of their elders and became unabashed in pursuing what they saw as Germany's national interest. They no longer try to be good Europeans at any price.

SCHMITZ: When you say this to leaders in Germany, do you have the feeling that anyone understands that historical background?

SOROS: Finance Minister Wolfgang Schäuble certainly does. He belongs to Helmut Kohl's generation. He is the last true European. That makes him a tragic figure because he understands what needs to be done, but he also recognizes the obstacles that stand in the way. He has to obey the Constitutional Court. He recognizes the intellectual influence that the Bundesbank exerts on the Constitutional Court, and that forces him to follow policies that he knows in his heart to be wrong. But I admire his honesty. He was the one who announced during the elections that Greece would need another bailout. That was the only time the euro crisis entered into the election campaign.

SCHMITZ: What do you consider to be Schäuble's biggest mistake in this crisis?

SOROS: His opposition to a genuine banking union, although I don't know what is Schäuble's responsibility and what is Merkel's.

SCHMITZ: Were you saying that the Spanish and Italian governments were not guilty of overspending, that the situation was fundamentally different from Greece?

SOROS: Yes. Spain actually had a better fiscal record than Germany, with big budget surpluses throughout the pre-crisis period. Spain was also a poster child of prudent banking regulation, increasing reserve requirements as the boom progressed. Its government debt started to rise only after 2008, when Spain insisted on pursuing countercyclical fiscal policy. As for Italy, its government deficits in the ten years from 1999 to 2008 averaged 2.8 percent of GDP, well within the Maastricht Treaty limit—and in the last year before the crisis, the deficit was down to just 1.7 percent. It was the steep rise in risk premiums that made Italy's debt unsustainable.

SCHMITZ: So in each country you have structural deficiencies, which were revealed by the crisis.

SOROS: Exactly, but the structural deficiencies are all different, so it is illogical and counterproductive to treat them all with the same medicine of budgetary austerity. The main thing all the debtor countries really have in common is that they are now in deep recessions from which they cannot escape because they are suffering from a permanent competitive disadvantage. As I've said already, the euro has created an uneven playing field by relegating debtors to the status of Third World countries that became overindebted in a currency they don't control.

SCHMITZ: But you always make it sound as if Germany is to blame for other countries' problems. Germany is the strongest country in the union, but it is not powerful enough to shoulder all responsibility alone.

SOROS: Whether German citizens and politicians like it or not, Germany is in charge of economic and financial policy. Germany cannot impose its will on the others, but no policy can even be proposed without first obtaining Germany's permission.

SCHMITZ: The German bailout obligations already amount to far more than $200 billion, roughly 85 percent of the German tax income. They could rise much higher. At what point would you admit that even Germany is overextended?

SOROS: Numbers like these, although they are widely quoted in German public debate, are completely misleading. There is very little risk of Germany having to pay vast sums to the other countries. They have suffered practically no losses so far. The alleged transfers have actually all been in the form of loans and guarantees; it is only if the loans are not repaid or if the guarantees are called that real losses would be incurred. In the German mind, there has been no clear differentiation between cash and guarantees. Most Germans believe that hundreds of billions have already been spent. However, only some $55 billion has actually been spent on aid packages for Greece; the rest of the supposed costs to German taxpayers are just potential liabilities in the framework of the European Financial Stability Facility (ESFS) and the European Stability

Mechanism (ESM). Guarantees have a peculiar character: the more comprehensive and convincing they are, the less likely they are to be invoked.

SCHMITZ: But would you agree that there is a feeling among Germans that they have done their share and the other countries haven't, and that's why they are so strict?

SOROS: Yes. Germany is afraid of becoming the deep pocket of Europe in a transfer union. That attitude has been fatal for the European Union. If you think about normal nation-states, every country is in some sense a "transfer union." It is always the more-productive, more-successful parts of a country that have to support the less-developed regions. The most successful areas generally—not always—tend to be urban, and so it's usually the urban industrialized regions that support the rural and backward regions.

SCHMITZ: So Germany is the prosperous region, and good leadership would require it to subsidize the other regions?

SOROS: Not subsidize, but equalize the cost of credit. Germany thinks it is showing good leadership by preventing a breakup of the euro and by insisting on stricter fiscal discipline. But in fact, it is not living up to its responsibilities by opposing the introduction of eurobonds. What it is really doing is the absolute minimum that is just enough to prevent a euro breakup—and always doing this at the last possible moment. Doing the minimum may prevent a collapse of the euro, but it will perpetuate a situation where debtor countries are at a permanent disadvantage. That is almost inevitable, as I've already said, because the debtor countries have to pay risk premiums to keep refinancing their debts, denominated in what is really a foreign currency—the euro. This puts them in the same position as the countries in Latin America after 1982, when they could not pay their debt denominated in US dollars. That led to a lost decade for Latin America, and Southern Europe now faces a similar fate. That is the reason we need eurobonds. Otherwise, we will have a Europe in which Germany is seen not as a leader but as an oppressor and exploiter. It will not be loved and admired by the rest of Europe; rather, it will be hated and resisted.

SCHMITZ: Aren't you exaggerating? We have all seen occasional pictures of Greek demonstrators comparing Merkel to Hitler and other distasteful displays—but we have not really seen major anti-German riots anywhere in Europe.

SOROS: I am talking about what is in store. Right now, Germany still deserves the benefit of the doubt. Germany has emerged as the imperial power, the hegemon of Europe, but the German public does not want to be in that position exactly because of the painful memory of Hitler. It is in denial and is unwilling to live up to the responsibilities and, yes, the liabilities that go with being an imperial power. That turns Germany into an oppressor and exploiter without being aware of it. I consider that a tragedy—a Greek tragedy like *Oedipus Rex* (no pun intended)—where the perpetrator is himself a victim of his own ignorance. But with the passage of time some German politicians will discover the advantages of their current position—if they haven't already—and they will start defending it. Then the hatred and resistance will be justified.

SCHMITZ: How could Germany avoid that fate?

SOROS: It has to learn what it means to be the first among equals. The Bretton Woods system made the United States first among equals, but it was eager for that role. That turned the country into a benevolent hegemon that earned the lasting gratitude of Europe. Germany could do the same by helping to resolve the euro crisis instead of obstructing any systemic solution, which is what it has been doing until now.

SCHMITZ: Can you give a concrete example of what you call this obstruction?

SOROS: Eurobonds are one example. Eurobonds are often compared with the Marshall Plan. Germans argue that the Marshall Plan cost America only a few percent of GDP, whereas eurobonds would cost a multiple of Germany's GDP. That argument is comparing apples with oranges. The Marshall Plan was an actual expenditure, but eurobonds would involve only a guarantee that would never be called upon. As I have said before, guarantees have a peculiar character: the more convincing they are, the less likely they are to be invoked. To provide such a guarantee is the historic opportunity that Germany is missing by holding the heavily indebted countries to their "*Schuld.*"

SCHMITZ: But again, why do you emphasize the role of Germany so much? Why is Germany always expected to provide guarantees and so on?

Soros: Because Germany is by far the most powerful country in Europe, and in a period of financial turmoil, it is the only one that is strong enough to provide the necessary guarantees. But also because up till now Germany has been the main obstacle that prevented other countries from going ahead with pan-European solutions such as eurobonds and a genuine banking union. Today, Germany does not have imperial ambitions, but paradoxically, the desire to avoid dominating Europe is part of the reason Germany has failed to rise to the occasion and behave as a benevolent hegemon. That puts before Germany a difficult choice: either lead the eurozone out of the looming depression with genuine burden sharing or leave the euro to the debtor countries—"Lead or Leave."

Schmitz: Are you serious in suggesting that Germany could "leave"? That would break up the eurozone, with unforeseeable consequences.

Soros: I am serious. From a strictly economic standpoint, the biggest problems caused by Germany leaving the euro would actually be in Germany. If Germany left, the euro would depreciate sharply and the debtor countries would regain their competitiveness. On the other hand, the deutsche mark would go through the roof. This would indeed help the adjustment process of the other countries, but Germany would find out how painful it can be to have an overvalued currency. Its trade balance would turn negative, and there would be widespread unemployment. German banks would suffer severe exchange rate losses and require large injections of public funds. On the other hand, the German government might find it politically more acceptable to rescue German banks than Greece or Spain. And there would be other compensations—German pensioners could retire to Spain and live like kings, helping Spanish real estate to recover.

SCHMITZ: But wouldn't leaving the euro be the end of the European Union?

SOROS: Not if it was done by common agreement that would preserve the common market. If Germany imposed trade barriers to protect itself from, for instance, cheap Italian imports, that would be the end of the European Union. But if dissolution took place within a single market, then Germany would have an adjustment problem but the EU and the euro could survive.

SCHMITZ: Merkel recently said in a speech: "I saw the GDR [German Democratic Republic] come down. I don't want to see that again in Europe."

SOROS: Yes, because she believes that the breakup of the currency would mean the breakup of the European Union.

SCHMITZ: You disagree?

SOROS: I do. In fact, you may have to break up the currency to *preserve* the EU. If Chancellor Merkel were really committed to preserving the European Union, the best way to do it would be by creating a proper banking union backed by pan-European guarantees and some kind of mutualized bond market. But if Chancellor Merkel is unwilling to make any further concessions to relieve the financial pressures created by the euro crisis, then the only remaining way to achieve the appropriate adjustment for the debtor countries would be by breaking up the currency. That would give the debtor countries a big one-time gain. You would actually turn the tables and make the debtor countries more competitive than Germany because the German mark would go through the roof.

SCHMITZ: But other countries like Belgium, Austria, the Netherlands, which used to be closely connected to the deutsche mark, would then leave the currency union, too.

SOROS: Yes, that is probably true, although it is not clear how well the Netherlands and Belgium would cope with their debt problems, which are as severe as the problems in some of the Mediterranean countries. Of course they could realign vis-à-vis the German mark before they formed a new currency block.

SCHMITZ: Still, the risk is that you would have a Northern Europe confronting a Southern Europe—an even more divided continent.

SOROS: Not at all. We would have two currency blocks within the European Union that could work better than a single currency. Both sides would have to cooperate to keep the exchange rates from diverging too much. That would actually be the fulfillment of Keynes's ideal of a currency system in which both the creditors and the debtors would be obliged to make adjustments in order to maintain stability.

Germany leaving the euro would bring instant relief for the debtor countries. Suddenly they would be so competitive that Italian and Spanish exports would be flooding the German market and creating unemployment in Germany. But excessive overvaluation would send the northern block into an economic depression. That, in turn, would force Germany to apply the classic Keynesian anticyclical policies that it currently opposes: cutting taxes, increasing public spending, and applying monetary stimulus.

SCHMITZ: The big question is: Where would France end up?

SOROS: In my opinion, France would become the natural leader of the Latin Europe. A currency division between north and south would put Germany and France on opposite sides. France would naturally fit in as the leader of the south, and Germany, of course, would be the leader of the Northern European or Protestant euro. The alternative, with France joining Germany in a northern currency union, is almost inconceivable. France could not face competition with Spain and Italy after a southern devaluation. By contrast, as leader of the Latin block, France would reassert itself as a great power. Britain could also resume its historic role as the arbiter between two continental blocks.

SCHMITZ: Speaking of France: when one talks to leaders in

Berlin, they paint France as "narcissist" and in denial about its difficult economic situation.

SOROS: They are right. Italy and Spain have actually addressed their structural problems, but France doesn't pay any serious penalty for failing to reform. It enjoys practically the same status as Germany as far as the cost of capital is concerned, whereas Italy and Spain have to pay a few percent of their GDP every year to refinance their debts. That has allowed the French government to avoid doing anything difficult or unpopular.

SCHMITZ: Basically, France is not being punished, and that's why the French are so hesitant to embrace reform.

SOROS: Now you are speaking like a German who admires the Spartan tradition. That reminds me of my father, who used to joke that Spartans are taught to suffer other people's pain without flinching. Unfortunately, that fits the current situation too well. But you are right. France hasn't really moved at all. And I don't see that changing anytime soon.

SCHMITZ: What do you think of Angela Merkel's leadership style?

SOROS: I think Merkel is an extremely skillful democratic politician who reads the mind of the electorate very well and represents the beliefs of the majority electorate very accurately. At the same time, she is pro-European in the sense that she is committed to preserving the euro. But there she is making a big mistake, because the euro is only a means to an end, which is a well-functioning European Union. As a result of the euro crisis, the means are now threatening to destroy the end. The euro, which was meant to be a stepping-stone on the path to a more complete political union, has already transformed the European Union from a voluntary association of equal states into a debtor-creditor relationship, which is neither voluntary nor equal.

Before the reunification of Germany, every country was in a minority; no nation or nationality was large or influential enough to dominate the European Union. But now Germany has emerged as the hegemon. That was not the result of an evil plot but the unintended consequence of a confluence of unexpected circumstances. As I have emphasized, Germany is a perpetrator that is the victim of its own ignorance. But with the passage of time, Germany may become hated and resisted as an exploiter, and the European Union may dissolve in acrimony.

SCHMITZ: That takes me back to your proposal that Germany should "lead or leave the euro." Well-known German economist Hans-Werner Sinn said you are playing with fire because you know full well that Germany cannot simply leave the euro, nor can it introduce eurobonds over the objection of the German Constitutional Court.

SOROS: But by generating the necessary political will the laws can be changed.

SCHMITZ: So the idea of having two zones within the euro

area is now more appealing to you than the idea of eurobonds that you pushed for earlier?

SOROS: Not at all. It would be far better for Germany to become a benevolent hegemon by agreeing to mutual guarantees in some form. The point I am making is that Germany must now choose: either become a benign leader, which means agreeing to a strong banking union and some form of eurobonds; or leave the euro and allow the debtor countries to mutualize their government bonds.

SCHMITZ: Eurobonds might equalize interest rates, but they are not going to do anything about competitiveness.

SOROS: Competitiveness is not the fundamental problem of the euro. Europe now has a large, probably excessive and unhealthy trade surplus with the rest of the world. Structural reforms like cutting government waste or removing restrictive practices will improve living standards in individual countries, but they will not correct the euro's basic design flaws. You need to do both.

SCHMITZ: Don't you think one of the problems of the euro was, or maybe still is, that it is overvalued?

SOROS: No, it's more complicated. The eurozone has ceased to be an optimal currency block. For the debtor countries, the exchange rate is too high. For Germany, it's too low. On balance, the euro is probably undervalued because of a lack of confidence in its durability.

SCHMITZ: So you think nowadays a depreciation of the euro is no way out for the weaker countries? Would such a step not instantly improve their competitiveness?

SOROS: Against the rest of the world, yes. Against Germany, no.

SCHMITZ: Which brings us back to the present approach of austerity and structural reform. Do you think the austerity policy that Germany is pitching can ever work?

SOROS: In the long run, yes. But as Keynes might have observed, in the long run it will kill the European Union.

SCHMITZ: What about the role of central banks, highlighted by the quantitative easing in Japan and the United States? The ECB is aspiring to a similar role as part of a solution to the euro crisis—but is the ECB becoming too powerful?

SOROS: The ECB's power greatly depends on Germany's support. At the height of the euro crisis, Chancellor Merkel had to turn to the ECB to save the euro. In the summer of 2012, the German government's representative Jörg Asmussen sided with ECB president Mario Draghi against the president of the Bundesbank, Jens Weidmann. That enabled Draghi to assert that the ECB would do "whatever it takes." But as soon as the financial pressures abated, Germany started whittling down the concessions it had made during the emergency. The ECB can try to act without the consent of the German government, but it won't get very far.

Schmitz: You have been so active in Eastern Europe, what is the perspective there on the European idea? Polish foreign minister Radosław Sikorski gave a speech a year ago in Berlin and said, "I may be the first Polish foreign minister to say that, but I want more German leadership."

Soros: The euro crisis actually hit Eastern Europe even before it became known as the euro crisis. In 2009, when the European authorities provided a guarantee for the financial system, this guarantee seemed credible. But the Eastern European countries, which were not members of the eurozone, were not in a position to provide credible guarantees. Therefore, the Eastern European economies were hit very heavily early on. But now, as the flaws in the construction of the euro became apparent, it's the debtor countries within the euro system that are suffering more, while Eastern Europe is relatively less affected. That is mainly because Eastern European economies are closely tied to Germany, and as a creditor country, Germany is doing substantially better than the debtor countries. Moreover, the Eastern European countries were never able to discount their government debts with the ECB. So they never had the benefit that the debtor countries in the eurozone are now losing—the dubious benefit of building up excessive debts at artificially low prices. Absolute debt levels in Eastern Europe are much lower, as befits countries that have had to borrow in foreign currencies.

Schmitz: If the Franco-German axis continues to weaken, as you are suggesting, could Poland be the new France?

SOROS: Poland has emerged as the soundest of the Eastern European countries in many ways. There is also a great determination in Eastern Europe not to become dominated by Russia and finally to fully participate in the eurozone. Poland's partnership with Germany could eventually come to rival the Franco-German alliance.

SCHMITZ: You have often mentioned how important self-criticism is for you. According to your writings, you have constantly reassessed yourself and tried to learn from your mistakes. When you look at the political leaders in Europe right now, for example, do you see that trait at all?

SOROS: Sadly, no. Political leaders are hampered from admitting mistakes. In other words, it doesn't get you any votes. I think Merkel has recognized, and in fact corrected, some of the mistakes she has made, but she doesn't like to boast about that. They have to be covered up because the public doesn't understand that making mistakes is human.

SCHMITZ: Is it possible that your analysis of the euro is all wrong?

SOROS: Of course that is possible. But I can't help believing in what I say, although I realize I may be wrong. I believe in my own fallibility. I take fallibility as seriously as Descartes took reason with his "*Cogito, ergo sum.*" Fallibility plays the same role in human affairs as mutation does in biology. The misconceptions and misunderstandings that go into our decisions help shape the events in which we participate. [See

Appendix.] Because we cannot base our decisions on perfect knowledge, we cannot avoid mistakes. There should be no shame or guilt attached to making mistakes, except when you persist even after you have realized that your policy is wrong.

Schmitz: Give us an example.

Soros: Suppose that the German public reads my book and finds my arguments persuasive; the German government would then be guilty if it did not reverse course. Only Germany is in the position to change the rules and resolve the euro crisis. If a debtor country tried it, it would be punished both by the European authorities and by the financial markets. Like it or not, the plain fact is that only Germany can end the nightmare that afflicts the heavily indebted countries, and therefore it is incumbent on Germany to do something about it.

Third Interview: Markets

GREGOR PETER SCHMITZ: Every time *Der Spiegel* publishes an interview with you, the standard comment of many readers is: "Why should anyone listen to the thoughts of an aggressive speculator on the global financial system who repeatedly undermined the stability of that system?"

GEORGE SOROS: Given the attitude to hedge funds in Germany, I am not surprised, but I should like to convince them that I understand the financial system better than some of the regulators who are in charge. I have been successful within the capitalist system. Who is better qualified to criticize the system than somebody who flourished within it?

SCHMITZ: Does it upset you when people call you a "speculator"?

SOROS: No, I do not mind that at all. As a matter of fact when I was given an honorary degree from Oxford and they asked me how I wanted to be described, I suggested "financial, philanthropic, and philosophical speculator." But they talked me out of it.

SCHMITZ: But speculation can upset markets and trigger instability.

SOROS: That is true and I recognize it. As far as my actions are concerned, I always play by the rules. I have always acted within the existing legal framework. So if my actions serve to undermine the stability of the system, it means that there is something wrong in the system that allows market participants, call them "speculators," to disrupt it. As a concerned member of society, I have spent a lot of time arguing that the rules governing the global financial system need to be improved. In doing so, I often suggest changes that may be detrimental to me as a speculator.

SCHMITZ: Really? Can you give us an example?

SOROS: In the United States, hedge funds spend a lot of money lobbying for lower taxes for their industry. I don't do that. In fact, I advocate for higher taxes, which would mean I would have to pay more. Nowadays, I can afford to stand up for principles. True, I cannot expect others to do the same. I did not always do it myself until I became rich.

SCHMITZ: But the perception many people have of you and your colleagues is very different. They blame speculators for the latest financial crisis in the United States or the euro crisis. Is that the reason you've decided to give billions of dollars to charity and your foundation?

SOROS: Do people think I am giving away money because I have pangs of conscience?

SCHMITZ: Isn't there some truth to it?

Soros: No, it is a total misconception. I have a clean conscience. The big events in which I participated would have occurred sooner or later, whether I speculated on them or not. For example, whether I had been born or not, the British pound would have been forced out of the European Exchange Rate Mechanism (ERM) in 1992. My talent has been to anticipate or recognize a coming wave, and to ride it, not to cause the waves.

Schmitz: But are you really such a little wheel as you claim? If you bet against gold or currencies, many other investors follow suit. You can definitely influence markets, for better or worse.

Soros: To some extent that's true. Since I became a public figure, the man who allegedly "broke the Bank of England," I have been cast as a financial guru who can influence markets. That has forced me to impose self-censorships on my statements—exactly because I can move markets.

Schmitz: Many scrutinize every single statement you make. Do you actually like that role?

Soros: No. It has made my life more difficult as an investor. My position changed after the sterling crisis. Before that, I did not have to concern myself with the effect of my statements on markets.

Schmitz: Are you truly so careful not to influence markets? For instance, cheap money—demanded by you publicly, in your role as a financial guru, as a recipe for the euro crisis—would also help you as an investor.

SOROS: That is true, but it would also help all other investors and, more important, it would help the EU. After nearly sixty years in the markets, I think I understand the financial system better than some of the people who are in charge of regulating it. So, as a concerned citizen, I feel justified in expressing opinions. I do not espouse policies in order to make a profit. I put public interest ahead of my private interests.

SCHMITZ: But when you speculated against the British pound, the United Kingdom had to leave the European Monetary System. That led to chaos in the markets while you made a fortune basically overnight.

SOROS: Look, even if I had not speculated against it, the British pound would have been devalued. There would have been a sterling crisis without me. When the markets are as large as they are in major currencies like the pound and the former deutsche mark, no single investor can have any lasting effect. If I had been the only one speculating, my speculation would not have been successful. I succeeded only because the rest of the market was doing the same thing. It was not my actions but Britain's policy of keeping the pound overvalued that led to chaos. More specifically, it was the policy differences between the British and German central banks that caused the crisis. I was merely better than others in detecting these differences and better in betting on it.

SCHMITZ: That is a very convenient excuse. Someone else

would have done it. How exactly did you try to improve the system in the case of your speculation against the pound?

Soros: I was not trying to improve the system. I was speculating that the pound would have to be devalued, and I was right. So I made money. If I had been wrong, I would have lost money. But a weakness in the system was exposed by speculators like me, and that is ultimately a good thing. The forced devaluation of sterling, which made me so famous, actually had a very beneficial effect on the British economy, as almost everyone subsequently agreed, including John Major and even his finance minister, Norman Lamont, and central bank governor Eddie George, who spent billions trying to fight off the speculation. In fact, Britain emerged from recession within months of the devaluation and then enjoyed its longest-ever period of steady noninflationary growth. I am not trying to take credit for helping the British economy in this way—I am just pointing out that, in this particular case, my successful speculation had a clearly beneficial result. To use a Marxist term, I shortened the birth pangs of an inevitable event.

Schmitz: Are you really retired? You are reported to have bet against the yen at the end of 2012 and allegedly earned more than $1 billion.

Soros: That was not me personally. My team handles my money. I still own the Quantum Fund but leave all management decisions to my managers.

Schmitz: Let's look more closely at this famous bet against

the British pound: in the months leading up to it, you borrowed as much as $10 billion—

SOROS: Correct.

SCHMITZ: What would have happened if you had lost big? You could not have covered all those losses, and chaos would have ensued in the financial markets, right?

SOROS: No, you are wrong. Because of the way the odds were set up, the amount of money I could have lost was well within my means and the only person who would have lost would have been me, and my investors.

SCHMITZ: But what would have happened to the money that was borrowed? Who would have paid that amount back?

SOROS: I would have had to pay it back. But the maximum that I could have lost was the cost of borrowing plus 2 percent, which was well within my fund's means. It was an asymmetric bet. That is why I could do it on such a large scale. If sterling had remained in the ERM, it would have had to remain within the prescribed trading band and could not have gained more than 2 percent. So, the most you could lose on a dollar would have been 2 cents plus interest. In the event, the pound was devalued by 20 percent, and those who bet against it made 20 cents on the dollar.

SCHMITZ: I understand that. I am just so insistent because when people are critical of short selling, they often cite your speculation against the pound as an example of an investor getting a lot of leverage with a relatively small amount of personal capital, so that he can influence markets. Don't you see that as a problem?

Soros: There is a problem with short selling, but my role in the sterling crisis is not a good example. Short-selling raids can sometimes destroy a financial institution or a currency that might otherwise be reasonably sound. Therefore, there should be rules against short-selling raids. But sterling was not sound in 1992; it was obviously overvalued and Helmut Schlesinger, the president of the Bundesbank, publicly said so at the time. It was his famous comment to this effect in the *Wall Street Journal* that actually triggered the breakup of the ERM in September 1992. So if any individual was responsible for the speculation against sterling, it was Dr. Schlesinger and his colleagues at the Bundesbank.

Schmitz: Still, in today's market circumstances, you say that there should be rules against short selling. What kind of rules?

Soros: I have argued for much tougher rules on credit default swaps, or CDS, a synthetic instrument that played a large role in the crash of 2008. CDS are toxic instruments whose use ought to be strictly regulated: only those who own the underlying bonds ought to be allowed to buy CDS. Instituting this rule would prevent the use of CDS in bear raids. But I was virtually the only one making this argument before the Lehman crisis.

SCHMITZ: If CDS are so dangerous, how could they have become so widespread in the first place?

SOROS: CDS came into existence as a way of providing insurance on bonds against default. But when these insurance policies were made into tradable instruments, they became bear-market warrants for speculating against a company or country. What makes CDS toxic is that such speculation can be self-validating because investors and even regulators believe that CDS prices convey information about the solvency of the underlying company or country.

SCHMITZ: What do you mean?

SOROS: The prevailing doctrine in finance today—called the efficient market hypothesis—says that the current prices of financial instruments always reflect the best available information about the future. If people believe this doctrine, then economic fundamentals start to move in response to market prices, as well as the other way round. This is the process I call "reflexivity," and it is one of the most important driving forces of financial markets and the world economy. Politicians, central bankers, and regulators who are steeped in the doctrines of rational and efficient markets—what I call the market fundamentalists—have until recently failed to recognize this process. [See Appendix.]

SCHMITZ: Can you be more specific?

SOROS: The CDS speculation before the Lehman bankruptcy, and also to some extent during the euro crisis, actually provides a perfect example of reflexivity. Because CDS were freely tradable market instruments, they came to be viewed by market fundamentalists, including regulators and the media, as well as many investors, as the best objective indicators of the default probabilities facing companies such as Lehman or countries like Spain. So when speculators piled into CDS and their prices shot up, as they did before the Lehman bankruptcy and again during the euro crisis, there was a perception that owners of Lehman Brothers or Spanish bonds faced much greater risks than they had previously recognized. That encouraged investors to dump bonds and shares issued by the banks or countries in question. And that, in turn, made it impossible for these banks or countries to raise new capital, just when they needed it most. In the case of sovereign nations, the mechanism worked not just through the sovereign bond markets but also through the domestic banking systems because many investors withdrew their money from Spanish banks and put it somewhere else because the rising CDS prices seemed to imply a rising probability that Spain might be forced out of the euro, and default. And those capital outflows meant, in turn, that the default and devaluation risks in Spain genuinely did increase. The key point here is that market speculation, essentially a bear raid that drove up the prices of CDS, actively increased the risk of default that CDS were supposed to passively reflect.

Schmitz: So the crash in 2008 and the euro crisis proved the destructive power of what you call this reflexive process?

Soros: Exactly. Financial markets deal not only with present reality, but also with the future—prices are a matter of anticipation, not information. Thus, we have to understand finance through a new paradigm that recognizes that financial markets always provide a biased view of the future, and that prices in financial markets may *affect* the underlying reality that those prices are supposed to reflect. This is the feedback mechanism of reflexivity. [See Appendix.]

SCHMITZ: Again, can you be specific about how this theory helped you to understand the events of 2008?

SOROS: Let me return to the CDS trade that triggered the disorderly bankruptcy of Lehman. With the help of reflexivity, the poisonous nature of CDS speculation during the crisis can be demonstrated in a three-step argument. The first step is to understand that being long and selling short in the stock market normally has an asymmetric risk-reward profile. Losing on a long position reduces one's risk exposure, whereas losing on a short position increases it. As a result, one can be more patient being long and wrong than being short and wrong. This asymmetry normally discourages short selling.

The second step is to recognize that the CDS market reverses the asymmetry of normal short selling. CDS offer a convenient way of shorting bonds where the risk-reward asymmetry works in favor of the bears. Going short on bonds by buying a CDS carries limited risk but almost unlimited profit potential. By contrast, selling CDS offers limited profits but practically unlimited risks. This asymmetry encourages speculating on the short side, which in turn exerts a downward pressure on the underlying bonds. The negative effect is reinforced by the fact that CDS are tradable and therefore are priced as warrants, which can be sold at any time, not as insurance contracts, which can be cashed in only in case of an actual default. That makes CDS contracts more valuable than insurance policies. This was dramatically demonstrated in the contest between Goldman Sachs and AIG (American Insurance Group). AIG sold CDS and Goldman Sachs bought them as warrants on a gigantic scale. The contest was won by Goldman Sachs. The day after the bankruptcy of Lehman Brothers, AIG, which was one of the world's best insurance companies, became effectively insolvent and had to be rescued by the US government.

SCHMITZ: But what is the relevance of reflexivity?

SOROS: That comes in the third step. Reflexivity tells us that the mispricing of financial instruments can affect the economic fundamentals that market prices are supposed to reflect. Nowhere is this phenomenon more pronounced than in the case of financial institutions, whose ability to do business depends on confidence in their solvency—what people call "trust." A sharp decline in a bank's share and bond prices can undermine this trust very quickly because it can increase the bank's financing costs to the point where it becomes genuinely insolvent. So bear raids on financial institutions can be self-validating. The euro crisis showed that a similar reflexive process can also undermine confidence in the solvency of sovereign governments, especially when they are locked into a currency system they cannot control.

SCHMITZ: So this self-reinforcing speculation was a cause of the global financial crisis—

SOROS: That's right. Financial institutions like AIG, Bear Stearns, Lehman Brothers, and others were, in my view, destroyed by bear raids. Shorting their stocks and buying CDS mutually amplified and reinforced each other. The unlimited shorting of stocks was made possible by the abolition of the "uptick rule," which previously hindered bear raids by allowing short selling only when prices were rising. The unlimited shorting of bonds was facilitated by the CDS market. The two made a lethal combination. CDS are ticking time bombs. Unfortunately, Warren Buffet and I were practically the only people making this argument.

SCHMITZ: Do you mean to say that AIG, Bear Stearns, and Lehman Brothers were fundamentally sound?

SOROS: No. But Lehman might have avoided a disorderly bankruptcy if there had been more time to find an alternative solution. That would have been less disruptive. And AIG failed almost entirely because of the CDS market. Its traditional insurance business was actually one of the soundest in the world. If it had not been for the mistake of treating CDS as insurance, not warrants, AIG would have been fine.

SCHMITZ: But what about the euro crisis? When we look at the euro crisis, what was the role of speculators in that crisis?

SOROS: They did not cause the crisis; they just exposed weaknesses in the design of the currency union. Those flaws would have been uncovered sooner or later. If you look at the speculative transactions—such as CDS in government bonds—

they had not increased dramatically in the run-up to the euro crisis. The stories about a concerted attack of US hedge funds against the euro are a myth.

SCHMITZ: Are you saying that the euro crisis was all the fault of politicians and had nothing to do with financial speculation?

SOROS: Financial markets did have a big influence. As I keep saying, financial markets don't reflect reality but help create their own distorted reality. Look at what happened when Chancellor Merkel insisted that the rescue of the banks should be the responsibility of each country individually. In retrospect, that was the first step in a process of disintegration. Had Merkel agreed to support the banks on a euro-wide basis, history would have taken a different course. There might have been no currency crisis, and the banking crisis, which is still acute today, might have been settled on the European level.

The markets didn't understand any of that. For about a year after the Lehman bankruptcy, interest rate differentials remained unrealistically low because the European Central Bank was still discounting government bonds on equal terms, so that the markets erred on the side of optimism. Then came the Greek shock, when the markets realized that Greece could actually default. Suddenly, the markets imposed very severe risk premiums on *all* heavily indebted countries, which therefore no longer had the fiscal strength to support their banks—and that was really the onset of the euro crisis. So, markets first failed to identify the flaws in the euro structure, and once they became aware of them, they overreacted. That shows that: (a) markets are not as rational and infallible as market fundamentalists like to believe, and (b) the markets played an active role in the crisis.

SCHMITZ: But your point is that politicians would have been able to control the markets if they had acted differently—

SOROS: I would say, *might* have been.

SCHMITZ: Everybody says we have to regulate the financial markets more. That sounds good, but is it realistic? Can one really tame the markets?

SOROS: There is a cat-and-mouse game going on between regulators and market participants.

SCHMITZ: Where, according to you, the mice—the market participants—often have the upper hand.

SOROS: That is because they get an extra boost from an exaggerated faith in the market's wisdom. That was the big misconception propagated by our national hero Ronald Reagan, who always talked about the "magic of the marketplace." That gave the market participants too much leeway. I call it market fundamentalism. I think it is better to have a cat-and-mouse game where the cat has the upper hand.

SCHMITZ: So you support stricter regulation and more control of the markets?

SOROS: Not exactly. I support *better* regulation and more efficient controls. However, you have to recognize that regulations will never be completely successful. They will always be full of holes. The mice will always discover new holes and the cats have to fill them. As I like to put it, markets are imperfect, but regulators are even more imperfect. Regulation should be kept to a minimum, but there has to be some cooperation between market participants and authorities, as was the case in the early postwar years. In that period, the Bank of England was a very successful regulator by cooperating with market participants. This clublike cooperative spirit was broken by the market fundamentalists.

SCHMITZ: So whom do you blame for the euro crisis? The politicians or the markets?

SOROS: I blame both and neither. As I explained in my recent article [see Appendix], all human beings base their decisions on imperfect understanding. That is the human condition. I call it the "human uncertainty principle," and I made it the cornerstone of my philosophy. That is in direct conflict with mainstream economics, which treats both market participants and regulators as if they had access to the best available information and applied it with total rationality.

SCHMITZ: How did you arrive at this view?

SOROS: I was struck by the intellectual incoherence of the orthodox economic theory even as an undergraduate at the London School of Economics. I was reading Karl Popper's

The Open Society and Its Enemies, in which he explained that the Bolshevik and Nazi regimes had something in common: they both claimed to be in possession of the ultimate truth. Since perfect knowledge is unattainable, that claim is false and can be enforced only by resorting to repression. Popper proposed an alternative form of organization: the "open society," based on the recognition of our inherent fallibility. Having experienced both the Nazi and Bolshevik regimes at first hand in Hungary, I became passionately devoted to the idea of open society. I studied Popper's theory of scientific method and started questioning the postulates of economic theory. That is how I built my human uncertainty principle on the twin pillars of fallibility and reflexivity.

Schmitz: And how was your theory received when you published it?

Soros: It became compulsory reading for fund managers and was taught in some business schools. But it was dismissed or ignored by academic economists. All that changed after the crash of 2008. The bankruptcy of Lehman Brothers was also the bankruptcy of rational expectations theory.

Schmitz: But how in practice does all this relate to the euro crisis?

Soros: The euro crisis was a direct consequence of the crash of 2008, and it is a case study of how reflexivity operates under what I call far-from-equilibrium conditions. The euro crisis revealed major flaws in the construction of the euro that the markets and the financial authorities had previously ignored. These intellectual misconceptions then reflexively changed the real world. First, reflexivity worked to amplify the economic strength of the eurozone, by encouraging investors to pour money into Spain, Greece, and Ireland, on the false belief that sharing a currency with Germany would mean these countries would also permanently share similar credit conditions. Then, from 2009 onward, the reflexive process went into reverse, as it usually does. In short, reflexivity created a boom-bust cycle that nearly destroyed the euro in 2011–2012 and may yet destroy the European Union, for the reasons we discussed in the second interview.

SCHMITZ: What exactly were the misconceptions that drove this boom-bust process?

SOROS: The most serious misconception, as I said in the second interview, was the failure to understand that member countries became indebted in what was in effect a foreign currency once they created an independent European Central Bank. Developed countries with their own central banks do not default, because they can always print money. Their currencies may depreciate in value, but the risk of default doesn't arise. By contrast, Third World countries that have to borrow in a foreign currency, like the dollar, run the risk of default. To make matters worse, such countries are exposed to bear raids. In short, the euro relegated the "periphery" to the status of Third World countries—and until 2009, almost nobody understood this.

SCHMITZ: What was the practical effect?

SOROS: Government bonds were treated as riskless throughout the eurozone. The regulators didn't require commercial banks to set aside any equity capital, and the European Central Bank discounted *all* government bonds on equal terms. This created a perverse incentive for commercial banks to accumulate the bonds of the *weaker* member countries in order to earn a few extra basis points. As a result, interest rate differentials practically disappeared among Germany and Spain, Ireland, and even Greece.

The convergence of interest rates caused a divergence in economic performance. The so-called periphery countries, Spain and Ireland foremost among them, enjoyed real estate, investment, and consumption booms that made them *less* competitive and created very large trade deficits. Meanwhile Germany, weighed down by the cost of reunification, engaged in far-reaching labor market and other structural reforms that made it *more* competitive and greatly increased its trade surplus. Those huge surpluses were partly created by selling cars, machines, and other industrial goods to Spain and the other debtor countries, financed by German savings for which there was no demand within Germany. This German credit poured into the peripheral countries on the false assumption that lending money to Spain was as safe as lending money to Germany, simply because they shared the same currency. This vast capital transfer continued for ten years, from the creation of the euro in the late 1990s until 2008. It was a private-sector market-driven process and had nothing to do with government decisions either in Germany or in the debtor countries—except, of course, the decision to create the euro itself. In the week following the Lehman bankruptcy, the capital flows suddenly stopped. The global financial markets literally collapsed and had to be put on artificial life support. This required substituting sovereign credit, backed by taxpayers' money, for the credit of the financial institutions whose standing was impaired.

SCHMITZ: Isn't that what the US government did?

SOROS: Yes, but European countries had to do something similar, too. Ireland was forced to provide public guarantees to all its banks, and even Germany felt obliged to follow suit. You may recall that in September 2008, money started flowing out of weak German banks into Danish banks, which were government guaranteed, and that prompted Mrs. Merkel to promise explicitly that she would not allow any German banks to go bust. This was the point when Europe should have acted together, but it did the opposite. Imagine what would have happened in America if all the US banks had to be supported independently by each of the American states. The EU should have used the financial crisis as the moment to take the next step forward toward fiscal and political union, but the political will was lacking. As we discussed earlier, the strongest resistance came from Germany, which did not want to become the deep pocket for the rest of the eurozone.

SCHMITZ: Do you think that German banks acted irresponsibly by lending to Spain, Ireland, and Greece?

Soros: They were forced to invest the country's surplus abroad. They couldn't keep all the Germans' savings in Germany because there wasn't any demand for it. I blame the authorities, more than the banks, for failing to understand the capital flows across the eurozone. The banks mostly played according to the rules that the authorities imposed.

Schmitz: Why did it take the financial markets so long to figure out the risks of channeling money from Germany to Spain, Ireland, and so on?

Soros: I think it was due to the rules that prevailed. First of all, the authorities treated all government bonds as if they were riskless. Secondly, the ECB was willing to lend to the banks against their bond holdings without limit, so there seemed to be no danger for the banks in continuing to hold even the weakest countries' government bonds.

Schmitz: Are you saying that the crisis was caused by *following* the Maastricht rules?

Soros: That is the tragedy of Europe: the European Union is now endangered by too much respect for the rule of law. We think of the rule of law as something that we all aspire to, but laws are fallible, like all human constructs. And when laws are based on faulty economic doctrines, the rule of law can do a lot of harm, especially if applied too literally, as it is at present.

Schmitz: Despite all the flaws you have described, the euro

is still pretty strong after four years of gloom and doom. Why is that?

SOROS: There was a time when the euro started falling quite substantially, which in the circumstances might actually have been beneficial to the European economy but was nevertheless disturbing to confidence in the euro's long-term prospects. At that point the Chinese took a stance, around $1.20 to the euro. They bought large amounts of euros because they were eager to preserve Europe as a market for their exports and were also eager to have an alternative to the dollar as a reserve currency. So it was really the Chinese who, for reasons of their own, helped to stabilize the euro around $1.20, and that turned out to be a very profitable speculation on the part of the Chinese authorities, because the euro is still well above $1.20.

SCHMITZ: Do you think the Chinese are still supporting the euro? Leading Chinese officials expressed anxiety about the developments in Europe.

SOROS: The Chinese may be less eager now to accumulate euros, but they are probably still protecting their past investments. The important point I would make here is that, actually, the largest speculators in the currency markets are the central banks. They are far bigger than hedge funds. Hedge funds flourish best by anticipating what the central banks are going to do.

SCHMITZ: Have the regulators now understood their errors

and corrected the rules that underpin the European banking system?

Soros: No. Very little has been done to correct the excess leverage in the European banking system. The equity in the banks relative to their balance sheets is wafer thin, and that makes them very vulnerable. The banks are also allowed to value their holdings of government bonds at par, and therefore, they don't reflect the losses hidden in their balance sheets. If the upcoming stress tests for European banks are real, they will reveal a tremendous shortfall in the capitalization of the banks, and that could provoke a new financial crisis. Alternatively, the stress tests would become a public relations campaign without any credibility.

Schmitz: Germany blocked stricter stress tests because the Germans were concerned about their own *Landesbanken*, which were severely overextended.

Soros: That's right. Although German politicians love to lecture others about financial prudence and rigor, it was largely because of Germany that the previous round of stress tests was a whitewash operation and had no credibility. Now that credibility should improve because the ECB is in charge of the 1,400 large banks that represent 75 percent of the total banking system. But the estimates are that if all the banks valued their assets correctly, there would be a tremendous shortfall—and it will be hard for the ECB to conduct truly rigorous stress tests unless there is money available for weak banks to be recapitalized. Unfortunately, that money is not available because Germany refuses to allow the ESM to be used for this purpose. This is ironic because the whole point of creating the ESM was to institute a pan-European mechanism to recapitalize the banks—and Chancellor Merkel strongly supported this idea in 2011.

SCHMITZ: So the issue in Europe is that banks still operate internationally, but fail nationally?

SOROS: Well, their operations were also increasingly national. And that started with Merkel's fateful decision to make each country responsible for its own banks. That set in motion a renationalization of the banks in the sense that they are now returning to their national silos, and instead of a euro-wide banking system, you will have each country with a separate banking system, which is really part of a process of disintegration.

SCHMITZ: So you are expecting another rift in Europe—between banks in the North and the South?

SOROS: The new divide is between the creditor and the debtor countries. You can speak of "North and South" for simplicity.

SCHMITZ: Are you suggesting that it was a mistake to force private investors from the North to write off their investments in Greece and Cyprus?

SOROS: It's a very controversial action because it retroactively makes government bonds more risky.

SCHMITZ: It's basically a retrospective change of rules.

SOROS: I think it's very unfair, not only toward the investors, but toward the countries that have become heavily indebted as a result of the way the euro was managed, rather than the way they were managing their own affairs. The one exception, as noted, is Greece, which genuinely abused the rules and cheated. And even in Greece, the people who did the cheating are not the people who are suffering today. The perpetrators probably have their money in Switzerland. But other countries, like Spain, were very good in managing their fiscal affairs and entered the crisis with lower debt ratios than, for instance, Germany. Because of the risk premiums that developed, though, they now have a lot more debt. So I think it's very unfair the way the bank bailouts have worked out—changing the rules now and making government bonds so risky, in retrospect. It may suit Germany, but it really does hurt the other countries.

SCHMITZ: Does it also undermine the stability of the market because it makes investors more reluctant to invest?

SOROS: They will certainly expect to receive higher interest rates in the heavily indebted countries.

SCHMITZ: Of course, many ordinary people would say it's about time that private investors experience losses as well, and it's not the government's responsibility to bail them out.

SOROS: That is understandable. But it is all about timing. It is simply the wrong time to introduce those new rules. It would have been a very good time to do it when the euro was introduced, but it didn't happen. Now it is happening retroactively. This favors Germany. There's no question about it. And it ensures that Germany will always be in a much better position than the other members of the eurozone. At the same time, it ensures that the eurozone as a whole will be mired in stagnation, and that is intolerable.

SCHMITZ: But average citizens are not very impressed by such arguments. They think bankers should be punished, and they don't trust financial markets.

SOROS: That mistrust is well placed. The very prestigious institutions on Wall Street pursue their self-interest without regard to the common interest. I have sympathy with the public anger, and with movements such as Occupy Wall Street, because many ordinary citizens are victims of Wall Street. Financial investors in Wall Street investment banks got the benefits when the banks made a profit, but when they lost a lot of money, the state was obliged to take over the losses. That was unfair, and people who lost their jobs have a legitimate complaint.

SCHMITZ: Aren't you contradicting yourself? On the one hand, you admit that the rules are unfair; on the other, you claim that changing them is unfair.

SOROS: I am, and I am aware of it. That's why I am arguing for eurobonds. That way nobody is punished retroactively, and going forward everybody will be playing on a level playing field.

SCHMITZ: But the German taxpayer would have to pay the debt of the others.

SOROS: Not under my scheme. All the existing government debt is converted into eurobonds, but each country remains responsible for its own debts.

SCHMITZ: So each country can resume its profligate habits.

SOROS: That is a misunderstanding. The conversion applies only to the existing debt. A European Fiscal Authority will allow only the refinancing of the existing debt. Any additional debt would be the sole responsibility of the issuing country, and financial markets, remembering recent history, will charge stiff risk premiums. That's a stricter discipline than what you have at present.

SCHMITZ: But what about the risk German taxpayers would be taking by guaranteeing the existing debt of other countries?

SOROS: It is negligible. It would occur only if a debtor country left the euro, but none of the debtor countries would have any reason to leave because they would have much better access to credit as members than on their own.

SCHMITZ: What about Germany?

Soros: It can decide to lead or leave. I am sure that if the Germans understood the full implications of their choice they would opt to stay and become a benign hegemon. The alternative is the nightmare in which Europe currently finds itself.

Schmitz: Let's come back to the globalization of financial markets. In the years before the financial crisis, roughly 40 percent of each Harvard senior class went to work in finance after graduation. Is that good or bad for a society if the most gifted graduates just want to make money?

Soros: The profitability of the finance industry has been excessive. For a while, 35 percent of all corporate profits in the United Kingdom and the United States came from the financial sector. That's absurd. The banking sector is acting as a parasite on the real economy, but the problem is that it is a parasite on the global economy, not on the national economy, making it a great export industry. The authorities in different countries still haven't made up their minds whether that is in the national interest or not.

Schmitz: The authorities in the United States have moved more quickly to ban proprietary trading than their counterparts have in Europe.

Soros: The United States hasn't been all that successful in that regard because there is still a serious problem with respect to trading in synthetic instruments, in collateralized debt obligations (CDOs) and CDS. This is a monopoly of five large banks, of which Citigroup, JP Morgan Chase, and

Bank of America are American; Deutsche Bank is German; and BNP Paribas is French. That oligopoly has not been broken up, because the banks successfully lobbied against it. So, proprietary trading has not been all that effectively reduced in America. In any case, proprietary trading does not have all that much to do with the present weakness of the European banking system.

SCHMITZ: Would you say the bigger problem is that the banks have not been broken up, that they are still too big? That is true on both sides of the Atlantic.

SOROS: The issue of "too big to fail" has not been solved at all. There are all these attempts at creating a resolution authority, but they are all for the future. Altogether, the authorities, particularly in Europe, have devised rules to avoid the next crisis, because they are introducing new rules in 2018 and 2020. But we have not solved the current crisis. I am now arguing that you need a genuine stress test, and based on the genuine stress test, you need to recapitalize the banking system now, because unless you do that, the banks will not lend to the real economy.

The ECB has been successful in pumping liquidity into the banks, but the liquidity doesn't leave the banks except to buy government bonds, primarily of their own country, because the banks can do so without setting aside any of their own equity. It is this set of regulations that encourages the banks to invest in government bonds. This has helped to bring down the risk premium on Italian and Spanish government bonds, but it has starved these economies of working capital. The banks are not willing to lend to industry—and particularly not to small and medium enterprises—because such lending would require them to set aside a lot of their capital. And the banks cannot afford to do this because they would then fail the stress tests. So this has created a credit squeeze that is particularly hurting Italy, and to a lesser extent Spain, and this is pushing those countries further down in terms of economic activity.

SCHMITZ: So failures in bank regulation are still crippling the European economy, but what about hedge funds? What do you make of Chancellor Merkel's idea to clamp down on hedge funds?

SOROS: It's the old habit of killing the messenger. It's catering to a popular prejudice. It doesn't solve problems. If it did, you wouldn't have the crisis.

SCHMITZ: Does the world really need hedge funds?

SOROS: I think that hedge funds are a very efficient way of managing money. But I clearly see the risks. Hedge funds use a lot of credit, and that is a source of instability. My conclusion is that all transactions should be regulated—hedge funds should not be singled out.

SCHMITZ: Now you sound like a person who would run into a police station and tell the officers: "Please, handcuff me—I am dangerous!"

Soros: Not at all! I think there needs to be appropriate regulation of the financial markets, but it is impossible to prevent speculation. There is very little difference between speculation and investment. Basically, the only difference is that investments are successful speculations, because if you successfully anticipate the future you make a speculative profit. And vice versa, unsuccessful speculations turn into investments. I don't have a bad conscience at all. I am very proud to be a successful speculator.

Schmitz: Speaking of the perception of speculators: People are still fascinated with you because they have a hard time figuring out if you are a villain or a saint. You have made billions investing in the markets—and you have given away billions. How do you see yourself?

Soros: Something in between. I certainly don't claim to be a saint. It's an unrewarding ambition—hard to live up to and no fun. John D. Rockefeller established his foundation in 1913, after he was accused of making monopoly profits. He hoped to improve his public image. It is different in my case. When I set up my first foundation in 1979, I had no public image, so I didn't need to improve it. I was a small fry in the market, managing a fund of merely $100 million. Then I had a fantastic run, making more than 100 percent profit in each of the next two years. I became personally richer than I ever wanted to be, but the tension associated with running the fund became almost unbearable. I had a kind of midlife crisis. That is when I decided to take philanthropy more seriously. At first I regarded it as a personal predilection, a hobby in which I could afford to indulge, but eventually it became both an obligation and a privilege because I was in a position to do things that few others could do.

Schmitz: How did you feel at the end of that day in 1992 when the pound was devalued? It had been a huge bet that turned out to be extremely profitable.

Soros: Well, it was bigger and more dramatic than other trades. But otherwise it was not so special. I am not even sure whether 1992 was a particularly good year for the fund. Whether I am speculating on the long side or the short side, there is always risk and tension, particularly if you use leverage. The tension is built into the profession; it's something that I had to live with every day. Maybe that day was a high point, but it was not all that different from the tension that I was living with all the time.

Schmitz: In biographies written about you, people have described you as being very cool, almost detached. Others have said you lost sleep over your investments. What is the truth?

Soros: The latter. Speculating was an enormous strain, and maintaining a cool demeanor added to the strain. You couldn't allow the market or the counterparty with whom you were trading to sense that you were in some way vulnerable because they would take advantage of it. So, you had to pretend to be cool. Some gambles have made me so agitated that I could barely walk or breathe.

SCHMITZ: You once told a friend that what you did was like playing monopoly as a child.

SOROS: That's true, but when I faced getting wiped out, I was forced to realize that running a hedge fund was no child's play. One day when I was running around trying to arrange for a credit line to cover a transaction I had just made, I thought I was having a heart attack. I realized that in trying to win a game, I was in danger of losing my life. That was the year 1979, when I decided to start my foundation. Once the foundation got off the ground, I became more motivated to continue making money in order to have more resources for the foundation.

SCHMITZ: What is your fear when you speculate?

SOROS: Fear of losing, of course.

SCHMITZ: But you have often said that you don't really care about money. Is that just you being coquettish?

SOROS: No. It is true. Otherwise I wouldn't give it away as easily as I do. Although I don't care for money as such, I'm engaged in a game. In order to play well, you have got to be engaged, you can't afford to lose. I used to suffer from backaches, but the backaches served to alert me that something was wrong in the portfolio.

SCHMITZ: In 2008, when a global crisis hit the financial markets, you took charge of your investment fund again after you had officially retired a few years earlier. Why?

Soros: Because I didn't want to lose the fortune that I had accumulated during a lifetime so that I could keep giving it away, and I felt that I was better qualified to deal with the looming catastrophe than others. So, I resumed control. That caused me a lot of tension and anxiety, but I felt better than if I had lost my fortune. I also gained a lot of experience, and it improved my understanding of markets. Being engaged in decision making really helps to sharpen your judgment. When I am distant from the market, my vision, my anticipation of the future becomes fuzzier. There is no substitute for being at risk to sharpen your vision.

Schmitz: You say you wanted to preserve your fortune so you could keep giving it away. But you earned billions of dollars in the crash.

Soros: Making money is the only way I know how to preserve my wealth.

Schmitz: Wouldn't you also personally miss something if you were to lose your fortune?

Soros: It depends on how much of it I lost. Obviously, if I lost everything, my standard of living would decline, but I haven't raised my standard of living to the level of my wealth—because I'm using most of it for the foundation. I think spending a lot of money just for the sake of showing off is a very wasteful way to live.

Schmitz: Why don't you just start a massive art collection like other billionaires, or amass airplanes or fine wine?

SOROS: Actually I have some very good art and fine wines in my home. I don't have a private plane because it would make me travel even more. But I find collecting alien to my nature because I have an abstract mind and collecting is the most concrete thing you can possibly do. It is not just a matter of buying a certain number of paintings or having a certain number of cars in your garage or wine bottles in your cellar. You also need to remember their names. That would exhaust me.

SCHMITZ: So you never feel the urge to just spend money for the fun of spending money?

SOROS: What I enjoy most is that in deciding how to live, I don't have to think about how much things cost. I don't count how much money I spend, but I don't spend much compared to my fortune. That's because I don't want to lose touch with reality.

SCHMITZ: Your father, who had a strong influence over you, returned from World War I with the conclusion that he never wanted to worry about money again. He just wanted to enjoy life.

SOROS: That is true. He compared money to luggage. The lighter you travel, the easier the journey. So he lived well with very little money.

SCHMITZ: So giving away billions of dollars for philanthropic causes is simply a way of making your father proud?

SOROS: I wouldn't overanalyze it. That is the way I am, and

he had a lot to do with who I am. If I hadn't made a lot of money, I would not be a philanthropist. I am primarily interested in ideas. But I hate to think what would have happened if I had not made a lot of money: my ideas might not have gotten much play.

PART 2
December 2013

Fourth Interview: Future

GREGOR PETER SCHMITZ: We talked a lot about the crisis of the European Union. With regard to the euro, though, isn't the worst over?

GEORGE SOROS: If you mean that the euro is here to stay, you are right. That was confirmed by the German elections, where the subject was hardly discussed, and by the coalition negotiations, where it was relegated to Subcommittee 2A. Chancellor Merkel is satisfied with the way she handled the crisis and so is the German public. They reelected her with an increased majority. She has always done the absolute minimum necessary to preserve the euro. This has earned her the allegiance of both the pro-Europeans and those who count on her to protect German national interests. That is no mean feat.

So the euro is here to stay, and the arrangements that evolved in response to the crisis have become established as the new order governing the eurozone. This confirms my worst fears. It's the nightmare I've been talking about, and there is little chance we'll wake up soon. As I keep saying, Germany is the only country in a position to change the prevailing order. No debtor country can challenge it; any that might try would be immediately punished by the financial markets and the European authorities.

Schmitz: If you said that to Germans, they would say: Well, we have already evolved a lot. We are more generous now and have modified our policy of austerity.

Soros: I acknowledge that Germany has stopped pushing the debtor countries under water. They are getting a little bit of oxygen now and are beginning to breathe. Some, particularly Italy, are still declining, but at a greatly diminished pace. This has given a lift to the financial markets because the economies are hitting bottom and that almost automatically brings about a rebound.

But the prospect of a long period of stagnation has not been removed. There is widespread agreement among all the financial institutions and experts, with the conspicuous exception of Germany, that the eurozone is threatened by deflation. The consensus includes the IMF, the US Treasury, and the ECB, excluding the Bundesbank and its allies. Opposition from the Bundesbank will prevent the ECB from successfully overcoming the deflationary pressures the way other central banks have done, notably the Federal Reserve. That's why the eurozone is facing a long period of stagnation. And that prospect has set in motion a negative political dynamic. Anybody who finds the prevailing arrangements intolerable is pushed into an anti-European posture. So I expect the process of disintegration to gather momentum. During the acute phase of the euro crisis, we had one financial crisis after another. From now on I expect a series of *political* rather than financial crises, although the latter cannot be excluded.

Schmitz: You say that current arrangements are intolerable. What exactly needs to change? What needs to be reformed?

Soros: At the height of the euro crisis, Germany agreed to a number of systemic reforms, the most important of which was a banking union. But as the financial pressures abated, Germany whittled down the concessions it had made. That led to the current arrangements, which confirm my worst fears.

Schmitz: As we speak, European finance ministers are concluding an agreement on the banking union. What do you think of it?

Soros: In the process of negotiations, the so-called banking union has been transformed into something that is almost the exact opposite. Instead of creating a European banking system, it reestablishes national silos. This is dangerous.

Schmitz: What's the danger?

Soros: The incestuous relationship between national authorities and bank managements. France in particular is famous for its *inspecteurs de finance*, who end up running its major banks. Germany has its *Landesbanken* and Spain its *caixas*, which have unhealthy connections with provincial politicians. These relationships were a major source of weakness in the European banking system and played an important role in the banking crisis that is still weighing on the eurozone. The proposed banking union should have eliminated them, but they were largely preserved, mainly at German insistence.

Schmitz: That is a pretty drastic condemnation. How do you justify it?

SOROS: In effect, the banking union leaves the banking system without a lender of last resort. The proposed resolution authority is so complicated with so many decision-making entities involved that it is practically useless in an emergency. Even worse, the ECB is legally prohibited from undertaking actions for which it is not expressly authorized. That sets it apart from other central banks, which are expected to use their discretion in an emergency. But Germany was determined to limit the liabilities that it could incur through the ECB. As a result, member countries remain vulnerable to financial pressures from which other developed countries are exempt. That is what I meant when I said that overindebted members are in the position of Third World countries that are over-indebted in a foreign currency. The banking union does not correct that defect. On the contrary, it perpetuates it.

SCHMITZ: You sound disappointed.

SOROS: I am. I left no stone unturned trying to prevent this outcome, but now that it has happened, I don't want to keep knocking my head against the wall. I accept that Germany has succeeded in imposing a new order on Europe, although I consider it unacceptable. But I still believe in the European Union and the principles of the open society that originally inspired it, and I should like to recapture that spirit. I want to arrest the process of disintegration, not accelerate it. So I am no longer advocating that Germany should "lead or leave the euro." The window of opportunity to bring about radical change in the rules governing the euro has closed. From now on, negotiations will merely be about changes at the margin.

The rules governing the euro used to be the primary focus of my interest, but that is no longer true.

Schmitz: So, basically, you are giving up on Europe?

Soros: No. I am giving up on changing the financial arrangements, the creditor-debtor relationship that has now turned into a permanent system. I will continue to focus on politics, because that is where I expect dramatic developments.

Schmitz: I see. Obviously, people are concerned about the rise of populist movements in Europe. Do you see any opportunity to push for more political integration, when the trend is toward disintegration?

Soros: I believe in finding European solutions for the problems of Europe; national solutions make matters worse. So I am hoping for some kind of pro-European political alliance emerging. There is a growing alliance of anti-European forces, and they will become an important element within the European Parliament, where I expect a significant anti-European minority after the 2014 elections.

Schmitz: Some people say up to one-third, right?

Soros: Yes. And I am particularly worried about the impact that the anti-European minority is going to have on the policies pursued by the so-called pro-European majority.

Schmitz: It seems the pro-Europeans are often silent on

important issues because they are afraid that speaking up might increase support for the extremists—for example, in the case of the Lampedusa refugees.

Soros: Like it or not, migration policy will be a central issue in the elections. We must find some alternative to xenophobia.

Schmitz: What do you propose to do about it?

Soros: I have established an Open Society Initiative for Europe—OSIFE for short. One of its first initiatives is Solidarity Now, in Greece. The original idea was to generate European solidarity with the plight of the Greek population that is suffering from the euro crisis and Greek solidarity with the plight of the migrants, who experience inhuman conditions and are persecuted by the Golden Dawn. It took us some time to get the project off the ground, and by the time we did, it was too late to generate European solidarity with the Greeks because other heavily indebted countries were also in need of support. So we missed that boat, but our initiative has had the useful by-product of giving us a better insight into the migration problem.

Schmitz: What have you learned?

Soros: That there is an unbridgeable conflict between North and South on the political asylum issue. The countries in the North, basically the creditors, have been generous in their treatment of asylum seekers. So all the asylum seekers want to go there, particularly to Germany. But that is more than they can absorb, so they have put in place a European agreement called Dublin III, which requires asylum seekers to register in the country where they first enter the EU. That tends to be the South, namely, Italy, Spain, and Greece. All three are heavily indebted and subject to fiscal austerity. They don't have proper facilities for asylum seekers, and they have developed xenophobic, anti-immigrant, populist political movements.

Asylum seekers are caught in a trap. If they register in the country where they arrive, they can never ask for asylum in Germany. So, many prefer to remain illegal, hoping to make their way to Germany. They are condemned to illegality for an indefinite period. The miserable conditions in which they live feed into the anti-immigrant sentiment.

SCHMITZ: Isn't it ironic that the nations suffering most from the euro crisis are also the ones worst hit by the migration problem?

SOROS: Indeed. The fact is that European migration policy is hopelessly outdated. It was established during the Cold War, when there was only a trickle of political refugees coming in from the repressive regimes of the Soviet empire. They were heroes of resistance and were genuinely welcomed. At the same time, countries such as Germany suffered from an acute shortage of workers.

But the world has changed, and there are now millions from all over the world who qualify as political refugees, and that exceeds the capacity of the European Union to absorb them. And today the heavily indebted countries of the South have an acute unemployment problem of their own.

Everybody is aware of the danger posed by xenophobic, anti-European parties that use the migration issue to get votes. Pro-Europeans like me find it more difficult to admit that our insistence on carrying out asylum policies to the letter of the law is just as biased and unrealistic as the uncompromising opposition of the anti-European forces. There is a crying need for a fundamental rethinking of both migration and asylum policy. The issue flared up after Lampedusa, but the European Commission postponed any meaningful discussion until after the 2014 European parliamentary elections to cover up the disagreement. This will yield the initiative to the anti-European forces. That is what I would like to prevent.

There are elements of a European migration policy that are already working. For instance, the EU is spending 2 billion on Syrian refugees outside European borders. Without that, Europe would already be flooded with Syrian refugees. Likewise, there is a very competent European emissary in the Horn of Africa, Alex Rondos, seeking to stem the flow of asylum seekers from Eritrea, but the public is not aware of it. We need a comprehensive strategy designed to relieve human suffering.

Schmitz: Looking at other European issues, aren't your foundations also very involved in the problems of the Roma (Gypsies)?

Soros: Yes, we have been engaged in those issues for more than twenty-five years. This is another problem that requires a European solution. All across Europe, the Roma face tremendous racism, discrimination, and hostile stereotypes. What is truly shocking is that their living conditions have actually deteriorated since they became EU citizens. At the same time, almost everywhere the majority population's attitude has become more hostile.

To address this, my foundations have focused primarily on education, but also on culture. One of our most important programs is the Roma Education Fund, which we established with the World Bank in 2005. In order to break hostile stereotypes, Roma children must be educated to take pride in their Roma heritage. That is a key part of our approach. Otherwise, educated Roma could blend into the majority population because they do not fit the negative stereotype, but the stereotype would remain.

If the approach developed by the fund were generally adopted, it would go a long way toward breaking the stereotype. The educated Roma themselves would become the most effective advocates in the struggle for equal treatment. That is already happening. We have managed to educate a small cohort of young Roma who retain their Roma identity. They are motivated, enthusiastic, and they are making a real difference. But there are too few of them and the Roma population is growing faster than the Roma Education Fund. The program ought to be scaled up by governments, with the help of the EU, and made available to *all* the Roma children in Europe.

This is another instance where the European Commission is playing a positive role. Structural funds help pay the additional costs involved in integrating the Roma. In the area of employment, which is of course also crucial, experts from the commission and my foundations are developing a demonstration project to make private-sector internships available to Roma youth enrolled in vocational schools. We are now working with the commission and the Council of Europe on the missing piece to a lasting solution of the Roma problem:

a European Roma Institute devoted to restoring Roma language, history, and culture.

SCHMITZ: What other European problems preoccupy you?

SOROS: British membership in the European Union. There is a real danger that Britain may be forced out or decide to leave. That would be a big step forward in the disintegration of the European Union.

SCHMITZ: Some people may say it wouldn't be a big loss. The British were opposed to the idea of a united Europe from the beginning. Why do you think it would be a big step toward disintegration?

SOROS: Because Britain has always played a balancing role between hostile blocks on the continent. And Britain's absence would greatly diminish the weight of the EU in the world. That would be a loss for the world. In my view, the world is suffering from a breakdown in global governance. There are many unresolved political crises that are causing many casualties and immense human suffering. That can be attributed to both Europe and America being preoccupied with internal problems and not pulling their weight in the world. I consider that one of the most harmful side effects of the euro crisis. The world badly needs Europe's soft power.

SCHMITZ: You said Britain might be forced out. Don't you think the British are kind of blackmailing the rest of Europe?

SOROS: Certainly. They have already gotten a lot of exemptions, and David Cameron, who I don't think wants to leave—

Schmitz: Because it would be bad for Britain, too.

Soros: I think it would be a big blow to Britain, because right now, Britain has the best of all possible worlds. It is part of the common market, but it is not part of the euro. Any change would be for the worse as far as Britain is concerned. But the anti-European forces, which I think are still a minority, are very active. The UK Independence Party has only 7 percent of the votes, but only 22 percent voted in the European parliamentary elections last time. If the same happens again, UKIP could capture one-third of the seats. And that would greatly reinforce the euro-skeptic wing of the Conservative Party.

Fortunately the Liberal Democrats, whose very survival as a national party is at stake, have decided on a strong pro-European campaign. There are now 2.7 million EU nationals living in Britain, the majority of whom would clearly want Britain to stay in Europe. That is something the OSIFE could do something about. We could mobilize the East Europeans living in Britain to vote in Britain. Many of them would choose the Liberal Democrats. That would make them a potent counterforce to UKIP and encourage both the Conservative and the Labour Parties to take a more pro-European position in the subsequent national elections.

Schmitz: We have discussed Britain. What about the other major European countries?

SOROS: Italy is the one I have been following most closely. The internal political problems there are more serious than generally recognized. The Italians used to be very pro-European. They looked to the European authorities to impose some discipline on their own politicians. When Mario Monti became prime minister, they rallied around him and he was able to assemble a really reform-minded government of technocrats. After a promising start, he failed to obtain any rewards from Chancellor Merkel and he lost momentum. It has been downhill ever since. The majority of Italians turned anti-European, and now that Berlusconi has finally been eliminated, Beppe Grillo, in spite of all his shortcomings, has the field all to himself.

The recent decision of the Italian Constitutional Court declaring the current electoral system unconstitutional will have far-reaching consequences. Effectively, it is the end of the second Italian republic. It is unlikely that the current parties will be able to agree on a new electoral law. That may extend the life expectancy of the Letta government, which is good news for the near term, but it means that the next elections will probably be conducted on the basis of the old electoral law and that is unlikely to produce a workable coalition. That is one of the future political crises one can anticipate.

SCHMITZ: Oh, that's very interesting. When we speak of political crises in countries, do you think in France, is it more of a political problem than a fiscal or economic one? Because they seem to be in denial.

SOROS: It's a combination of both. France is the sick man of

Europe. It has been exempted from penal risk premiums on account of its close association with Germany; nevertheless, its economic performance is inferior to that of Italy and Spain. It's a very depressing atmosphere in Paris. There is a mood of despondency. That will benefit Marine Le Pen, who is a more skillful politician than her father and is now expected to win the largest number of votes in the European parliamentary elections.

SCHMITZ: There is a new book out by Helmut Schmidt, the former German chancellor, and he accused Merkel of neglecting the relationship with Paris. He was saying: When I was in government, I had the relationship with Giscard d'Estaing. Later, it was Kohl and Mitterrand, and now she would have to make more of an effort to reach out to François Hollande and do something together with the French. Do you agree?

SOROS: Well, I think that has already happened. At first Hollande tried to distance himself from Merkel, but he has come to realize that he cannot afford to do so. He became an obedient junior partner—more junior than his predecessors. That has contributed to the mood of despondency in Paris.

SCHMITZ: It is interesting that you have a paralyzed government at home, but in foreign policy, Hollande is pretty active, right? That's a contradiction in a way.

SOROS: Not really. Actually, it's complementary, because foreign policy is the only place where Hollande can actually do something that appeals to the public.

SCHMITZ: Right, right. You said in the second interview that Poland could emerge as a junior partner of Germany.

SOROS: I can repeat what I said then, namely, that the new Europe as exemplified by Poland is much healthier both politically and economically than the old Europe. Hungary is an exception.

SCHMITZ: In the past week or so, we all saw the pictures from Ukraine, where people are very pro-European and want to join the European Union. That is in striking contrast to people in Greece, Italy, and France, who seem to be fed up with it.

SOROS: Well, that shows how important it would be for Europe to revive and to recapture the original idea of the European Union. Ukraine is a powerful reminder. You might call it a wake-up call.

SCHMITZ: What do you think of the current policy of the European Union in that region? Do you think they made mistakes by not offering more to these countries?

SOROS: The neighborhood policy is the prime victim of the Euro crisis. The EU has very little to offer because of its internal political and financial problems.

SCHMITZ: So Vladimir Putin had 20 billion to offer and the EU a few million?

SOROS: Well, that was in response to a pretty blatant attempt at extortion by President Yanukovych. That has backfired, but the spontaneous reaction of the Ukrainian people shows the attraction that Europe still has for the neighboring countries.

SCHMITZ: What do you think is going to happen in Ukraine?

SOROS: I don't like to make short-term predictions because they can easily prove to be wrong. I prefer to pontificate about long-term trends because, as Keynes said, in the long term we are all dead. But I will take a chance.

We have just witnessed a dramatic test of strength between Russia and the European Union. Russia came out ahead. That should be a wake-up call for Europe. At the same time the spontaneous uprising of the Ukrainian people showed Putin the limits of *his* power. In that contest, the Ukrainian people came out ahead. The net result is a stalemate and a continuation of the status quo in Ukraine. A corrupt, inept, and unpopular government is pitted against civil society, and neither side is able to impose its will on the other. Ukraine remains precariously balanced between Russia and Europe. Russia has gained the upper hand for the next two years at the cost of 20 billion and a significant concession on the price of natural gas. These funds will be wasted on keeping Yanukovych in power without any prospect for structural reforms that could make Ukraine economically viable. At the same time, Putin has to realize that his dream of reconstituting what is left of the Soviet Union through a customs union is unattainable. And civil society will have to struggle to preserve what it can of the freedoms temporarily regained by the uprising. The outlook beyond 2015 remains wide open.

SCHMITZ: Tell us a little more about the situation in Ukraine, because you know the country better than probably anyone else.

SOROS: Unfortunately, I am very out of touch. I used to know the Ukraine intimately. I set up a foundation even before Ukraine became independent, and it became an integral part of civil society. Putin accused me of being the instigator of the "color revolutions," but that was a false charge. Civil society was responsible for the color revolution, just as it is for the recent uprising. Still, this is the first time I have become totally out of touch. All my information has been coming from the foundation after a time lag. They told me a couple of interesting things. One is that the opposition to Yanukovych came not only from western Ukraine but also from the Russian-speaking East. A deeply divided country was unusually united. The other is that before going into recess, the Duma passed a law giving amnesty to the participants in the uprising. Now, it would be important to end the uprising on that positive note so as to preserve the capacity of civil society to protect itself.

SCHMITZ: What do you think the Europeans could have done differently?

SOROS: Of course, visa-free travel was a very important issue, and I think getting hung up on the Yulia Tymoshenko case was a mistake, because the EU was asking for too much and offering too little, practically nothing compared to Russia.

SCHMITZ: Do you think it would have been a good idea to offer membership to Ukraine early on?

SOROS: Ukraine is obviously very far from being qualified, and unfortunately, the European Union has lost the ability to offer membership because it is itself in a process of disintegration. This has greatly reduced its influence in the world. The same thing has happened in the case of Turkey.

SCHMITZ: What do you think of Putin's policy?

SOROS: Now you are coming to the crux of the matter. Russia is emerging as a big geopolitical player, and the European Union needs to realize that it has a resurgent rival on its east. Russia badly needs Europe as a partner, but Putin is positioning it as a rival. There are significant political forces within the Russian regime that are critical of Putin's policy on that score.

SCHMITZ: Can you be more specific?

SOROS: The important thing to remember is that Putin is leading from a position of weakness. He was quite popular in Russia because he restored some order out of the chaos. The new order is not all that different from the old one, but the fact that it is open to the outside world is a definite improvement, an important element in its stability. But then the prearranged switch with Dmitry Medvedev from prime minister to president deeply upset the people. The regime felt existentially threatened by the protest movement. Putin became repressive at home and aggressive abroad. That is when Russia started shipping armaments to the Assad regime in Syria on a massive scale and helped turn the trend against the rebels. The gamble paid off because of the preoccupation of the Western powers—the United States and the EU—with their internal problems. Barack Obama wanted to retaliate against the use of chemical weapons, but the British Parliament voted against participating. Obama got cold feet and, Hamlet-like, left the decision to Congress. He was about to be rebuffed when Putin came to the rescue and persuaded Assad to voluntarily surrender his chemical weapons. That was a resounding diplomatic victory for him. He then prevailed against the European Union in Ukraine. Yet the spontaneous uprising of the Ukrainian people must have taught Putin that his dream of reconstituting what is left of the Soviet Union is unattainable. He is now facing a choice between persevering or changing course and becoming more cooperative abroad and less repressive at home.

SCHMITZ: Do you see any shift in German policy toward Russia? We had a very strong relationship with Putin under Gerhard Schröder. Merkel has been far more confrontational. For example, she spoke out rather strongly against Putin in Vilnius.

SOROS: Well, having grown up in East Germany, she should have an inside understanding of Russia. The rapprochement with Poland has also created a less pro-Russian attitude in Germany. At the same time, Germany continues to make special deals with Russia. Russia has benefited from the fact that Europe is disunited. But now that Russia is emerging as a threat to Europe, it may once again become a force that brings Europe closer together. I pin my hopes on Chancellor Merkel.

SCHMITZ: How can you reconcile that with all your criticism of the Chancellor?

SOROS: I can't. But one must never give up hope. I have learned from experience that people can change when you least expect it. Think of the Burmese dictator Than Shwe, who gave up power after twenty years, just when things were going from bad to worse in Burma.

SCHMITZ: Could Ukraine be a wake-up call for Angela Merkel?

SOROS: Absolutely. I just read a report in *Le Monde* about a dinner at the European Council, which shows that she was definitely affected by it.

SCHMITZ: Is Russia a credible threat to Europe if its economy is as weak as you say?

SOROS: The oligarchs who control the Russian economy don't have any confidence in the regime. They send their children and money abroad. That is what makes the economy so weak. Even with oil over $100, which is the minimum Russia needs to balance its budget, it is not growing. Putin turned aggressive out of weakness. He is acting in self-defense. He has no scruples, he can be ruthless, but he is a judo expert, not a sadist—so the economic weakness and the aggressive behavior are entirely self-consistent.

SCHMITZ: How should Europe respond to it?

SOROS: It needs to be more united. Putin prides himself on being a geopolitical realist. He respects strength and is emboldened by weakness. Yet there is no need to be adversarial. The European Union and Russia are in many ways complementary; they both need each other. There is plenty of room for Russia to play a constructive role in the world, exactly because both Europe and the United States are so preoccupied with their internal problems.

SCHMITZ: How does that translate into practice, particularly in the Middle East?

SOROS: It has totally transformed the geopolitical situation. I have some specific ideas on this subject, but it is very complicated. I can't possibly explain it in full because there are too many countries involved and they are all interconnected.

SCHMITZ: Give it a try.

SOROS: I should start with a general observation. There are a growing number of unresolved political crises in the world. That is a symptom of a breakdown in global governance. We have a very rudimentary system in place. Basically, there is only one international institution of hard power: the UN Security Council. If the five permanent members agree, they can impose their will on any part of the world. But there are many sovereign states with armies; and there are failed states that are unable to protect their monopoly over the use of lethal force or hard power.

The Cold War was a stable system. The two superpowers were stalemated by the threat of mutually assured destruction, and they tried to restrain their satellites. So wars were fought mainly at the edges. After the collapse of the Soviet Union, there was a brief moment when the United States emerged as the undisputed leader of the world. But it abused its power. Under the influence of the neocons, who argued that the United States should use its power to impose its will on the world, President George W. Bush declared war on terror in response to 9/11 and invaded Iraq on false pretenses. That was a tragic misinterpretation of the proper role of hegemonic or imperial power. It is the power of attraction—soft power—that ensures the stability of empires. Hard power may be needed for conquest and self-protection, but the hegemon must look after the interests of those who depend on it in order to secure their allegiance instead of promoting only its own interests. The United States did that very well after World War II, when it established the United Nations and embarked on the Marshall Plan. But the neocons forgot that lesson. President Bush destroyed American supremacy in no time. The neocons' dream of a "new American century" lasted less than ten years. So did Hitler's 1,000-year Reich.

SCHMITZ: What's the connection?

SOROS: They each had a false idea, which they tried to impose by force—President Obama then brought American policy back to reality. His record in foreign policy is better than generally recognized. He accepted the tremendous loss of power and influence and tried to "lead from behind." In any case, he is more preoccupied with domestic than foreign policy. In that respect America is in the same position as Europe, although for different reasons. People are inward-looking and tired of war.

The world is now full of hegemonic powers that are unwilling to accept the responsibilities and liabilities that go with soft power. China is also a reluctant hegemon, and says: We are a developing country preoccupied with our own problems—we cannot afford to look after the problems of the world. At the same time, the Chinese harbor imperial ambitions. And there are many other developing countries that are aspiring to imperial power. A tension between soft and hard power seems to be characteristic of all actual or potential hegemons. This is the general background against which the Arab Spring is unfolding.

The Arab Spring has many similarities with the revolution that swept away the Soviet Union, but there are some major differences. The people of the Soviet empire were attracted to the West. Most of the Arab revolutionaries are mistrustful of the West and are fired by Islamic religious fervor. To complicate matters, there is a growing split between Shia and Sunni, and an effort by the Sunni monarchies to exterminate the Muslim Brotherhood.

As we have seen, the Western powers have turned inward. This has created a power vacuum, which has allowed conflicts to fester unresolved all over the world. Recently, Russia has moved into this power vacuum, trying to reassert itself as a geopolitical player. That was a bold maneuver, inspired by Putin's internal weakness, and it is paying off because of the weakness of the West. That is radically changing the geopolitical landscape. Suddenly, the prospect of a solution has emerged for the three major unresolved conflicts in the Middle East—Palestine, Iran, and Syria—when one would have least expected it. Russia can do what the Western powers couldn't because of the implacable opposition of Russia: achieve a political settlement in Syria.

The Syrian crisis is by far the worst, especially in humanitarian terms. Russia's entry as a major supplier of arms, coupled with Hezbollah's entry as a supplier of troops, has turned the tables in favor of Assad. The fighting can be brought to an end only by a political settlement imposed and guaranteed by the international community. Without it, the two sides will continue to fight indefinitely with the help of their outside supporters. Putin could force the Assad side to "voluntarily" surrender its chemical weapons. The rebel forces are less easily controlled by their outside supporters, and Putin may find it advantageous to let the fighting drag on, thereby keeping the price of oil high—his budget would fall into deficit with oil below $100. This raises the specter of a humanitarian catastrophe. Assad has followed a deliberate policy of denying food and destroying the medical system as a way of subduing the civilian population. Unless humanitarian assistance can be delivered across battle lines, more people will die from illness and starvation during the winter than from actual fighting.

Schmitz: What is the solution?

Soros: International public opinion is surprisingly complacent. It responds to natural disasters but tends to shy away from man-made ones. My foundations and I are actively involved in trying to raise public consciousness of the impending humanitarian catastrophe. The public can exercise pressure on governments to live up to their responsibility to impose a political settlement and ensure the delivery of humanitarian aid across battle lines during the negotiations. It can also provide material support to those who are already actively delivering aid across battle lines.

SCHMITZ: What about Iran?

SOROS: There has been an actual breakthrough in the Iranian crisis in the form of a temporary agreement on nuclear weapons. The smart sanctions imposed by the Western powers have been very effective. The Iranian revolution itself advanced to the point where it fell into the hands of a narrow clique, the Revolutionary Guard; the mullahs have been pushed out of power. As head of the mullahs, the ayatollah cannot be pleased. He must also be aware that the large majority of the population is profoundly dissatisfied with the regime. In contrast with previous attempts at negotiations, he seems to be in favor of reaching an accommodation with the United States. That favors the prospects for a final agreement.

SCHMITZ: That leaves the longest-lasting crisis, Palestine.

SOROS: Recent developments in Egypt have improved the chances of progress in the long-festering Palestinian crisis. The army, with the active support of Saudi Arabia and the Gulf states, has removed the legally elected president and is engaged in the brutal suppression of the Muslim League. This otherwise disturbing development has a potentially benign side effect: it raises the possibility of a peace settlement between the Palestinian authority and Israel, to the exclusion of Hamas. This would have been inconceivable a few months ago. Secretary of State John Kerry became engaged in the Palestinian negotiations well before this window of opportunity opened, so he is ahead of the game. Prime Minister Benjamin Netanyahu is very suspicious but cannot openly oppose negotiations because, having campaigned against Obama in the American elections, he holds a weak hand. Negotiations are making progress, but very slowly indeed.

If all three crises were resolved, a new order would emerge in the Middle East. There is a long way to go because the potential losers in one conflict may act as spoilers in another. Netanyahu, for instance, is dead set against a deal with Iran. Nevertheless, the broad outlines of a potential new order can already be discerned. Russia could become more influential, relations between Saudi Arabia and the United States may become strained, and Iran may emerge as America's closest ally, second only to Israel. But the situation remains fluid and may change from one day to the next.

SCHMITZ: We haven't discussed China.

SOROS: That's another long story. China is facing a tremendous problem. It has to change its growth model, which has been exhausted. It's not something that has to happen immediately, but it's already too late to have a smooth transition, because—let me explain.

The growth has been driven by exports and investments. China maintained an artificially low exchange rate that created an export surplus that the central government could use for its own purposes. That was a brilliant way of imposing taxation without representation and without the people actually noticing it. The fruits of their labor were collected by the central government through the artificial exchange rate. The proceeds were then used by the central government for investment. By not consuming but investing, the economy could grow at a very rapid rate. The growth rate effectively exceeded 10 percent a year. This occurred at a time when the Japanese economy, which had gone through a similar period of rapid growth previously, was undergoing a very painful correction and wasn't growing at all. So during this period China doubled every seven years and Japan remained stagnant. China outstripped Japan and became the second-largest economy of the world, and if it were to continue at that rate, it would outstrip the United States in a few more years.

But that won't happen. The household sector that was supporting this growth has shrunk, while the investments and exports have kept growing as a percentage of the total economy. Consumption takes up 70 percent of the GDP in the United States. In China, it's now down to 34 percent; investments and exports take up the rest. It was really the forced savings of the household sector, the ordinary people, through the artificially low exchange rate and negative real interest rates for savings, that was the motor of growth.

But the productivity increases produced by these very large investments were gradually shrinking and eventually the marginal return on investments turned negative. Profit margins on exports became razor thin. This created a situation where the growth could no longer be subsidized by savings and had to be supported by borrowing. That was a nonlinear process, which went parabolic in the last few years. According to some estimates, one unit of growth now requires seven units of debt, and total social debt has reached 250 percent of GDP. In other words, China experienced a boom or bubble that eerily resembled the conditions that preceded the financial crisis of 2007–2008 in the United States. Indeed, the bubble was more pervasive, because in the United States it was confined to the housing sector, whereas in China it involved the entire economy.

SCHMITZ: I remember you said in the third interview that it is very unusual that you have two crises in one single decade. Normally, a generation goes by until we see a similar crisis.

SOROS: Yes. People who lived through that experience recognized the resemblance and warned against an impending financial crisis in China. The financial authorities in Beijing actually took notice of this warning and decided to forestall the financial crisis by restricting credit growth. That is when the private sector developed ways to sidestep the official limits, and a shadow banking industry grew up at a remarkably fast pace. State-owned banks and others set up off balance-sheet subsidiaries called wealth management companies, and they engaged in unsound practices that were nevertheless accepted by the public, because there was an implicit guarantee by the state, similar to Fannie Mae and Freddie Mac in America.

But there is a fundamental difference. Both China and America have a political system and a market system. But in America, the market dominates the politics, whereas in China, the state and party system controls the market. China has allowed a market system to develop, but the state still retained partial ownership and total control of the economy.

SCHMITZ: Do you see that changing at all?

SOROS: Well, no, because the party wants to remain in power, although ownership is being gradually transferred from the state to party members. The People's Bank of China started restricting official credit in 2011. This led to the explosive growth of shadow banking in 2012–2013. In July 2013, a sudden jump in short-term interest rates to double digits threatened to push the real economy into a recession, and the party leadership pushed the panic button. It ordered the steel industry to restart the furnaces, and the PBOC to relax credit. The economy turned on a dime, and by November, when the Party Congress took place, it was already accelerating. The president then announced a series of far-reaching economic reforms, including a free trade zone for financial markets in Shanghai. There were political reforms as well, notably, forced labor was abolished and the residential permit (*houkou*) system was modified. President Xi Jinping took personal charge of economic reforms and the security services.

SCHMITZ: Do you think that is a sustainable model?

SOROS: No, it's not. When the leaders ordered the restarting of the furnaces, they also restarted the credit growth at an accelerating rate. That's unsustainable.

SCHMITZ: How long can it be sustained?

SOROS: That's the big unknown. We are in uncharted territory. The authorities were right in deciding that they can only introduce these structural reforms when the economy as a whole is growing, as opposed to the European authorities that insisted on structural reforms in the midst of austerity. But nobody knows how much debt a state-controlled economy can accumulate before it collapses, and nobody knows what form the collapse will take. Because the party is determined not to lose power, I suspect that it will abandon market reforms before it abandons growth, because a recession would cause social unrest. But rising inequality and the endemic corruption could also result in social unrest. So success is far from assured. How the internal contradictions are going to be resolved is one of the most important questions confronting the world today. That is why I have switched my focus from the euro to China.

SCHMITZ: What does that mean for Europe?

SOROS: Very little for the next couple of years. It's a longer-term problem.

SCHMITZ: There was a summit between the EU and China a few weeks ago, and it seemed like the Chinese were still very interested in Europe.

SOROS: Certainly, China wants to preserve Europe as a market for their exports and the euro as an alternative reserve currency. As you know, China intervened in the euro at $1.20 to the dollar, and that was the low point of the euro since then. In that respect, the attitude of China hasn't changed, but its capacity to invest in Europe may be impaired. The Chinese have accumulated something like $3 trillion of reserves, but they will need them at home to take over the bad debts accumulated in the hands of the local authorities and to recapitalize the banks that are now loaded with bad debt. They are also more interested in investing in sources of raw material, like iron ore. That will take priority over investing in Europe.

SCHMITZ: Would you say that they are still committed to propping up the euro, as they did in the last crisis?

SOROS: I doubt it. The euro has a tendency to appreciate, but it is not coming from China. It may come from other Asian countries like Japan, which is creating a lot of yen through quantitative easing. That is a negative for Germany, which is directly competitive with Japan in 75 percent of its exports.

SCHMITZ: Do you think that the Obama administration is right in pivoting from Europe to Asia?

SOROS: Well, Europe is just now entering a long period of stagnation that Japan is determined to break out of.

SCHMITZ: So you are basically saying that it is something that the Europeans have to come to terms with, that they are not as important to the Americans as they were in the past?

SOROS: That is the reality.

SCHMITZ: What do you think of the American economy?

SOROS: I'm as optimistic as the rest of the world. Where I am more optimistic is on the political outlook. I think the Tea Party has carried its opposition to Obama to an extreme that the American public will not support. The conservative establishment of the Republican Party will have to break with the Tea Party. This augurs well for a return to the two-party system where both parties try to capture the middle ground.

SCHMITZ: This brings us to the trans-Atlantic relationship. That relationship has been poisoned by the National Security Agency revelations. Do you understand the anger in Europe?

SOROS: I sympathize with it. The extent of the surveillance was a shock for the European public, and I think it's also a shock for Americans.

SCHMITZ: Are you disappointed that President Barack Obama is continuing these programs?

SOROS: He thinks that as a Democrat he cannot look weak on security, but he is making a mistake. Edward Snowden was a whistle-blower who exposed an excessive use of state power. I disagree with Snowden on that point. I believe that security should trump privacy. So I was ill-disposed toward Snowden at first when he flew to Hong Kong and then to Moscow. But I was shocked by the extent of the undisclosed surveillance, and Snowden gave a very credible defense that he did not allow any secrets to fall into the hands of the Chinese or the Russians.

SCHMITZ: Many compare him to Daniel Ellsberg, who leaked the Pentagon Papers about Vietnam. Ellsberg stayed in the United States, though, and faced the consequences.

Soros: Those were different times. Ellsberg was not afraid of being prosecuted, but I think Snowden had reason to fear that he would be. Look at the way the Obama administration treated WikiLeaks informant Bradley Manning, who was first held in solitary confinement and eventually condemned to life in prison.

Schmitz: Would you call Snowden a hero?

Soros: I respect him, and I would love to have him as an adviser of the US government in how to correct the excesses of the military. Actually, I would be happy to have him work for my foundation as an adviser so that we could be more effective in our critique of the Obama administration's surveillance policies.

Schmitz: You have developed theories on the financial market and on philosophy for a long time, but you were not really taken seriously by economists and by philosophers. You even referred to yourself as a "failed philosopher." But ever since the outbreak of the global financial crisis, which you largely predicted, your theories are in vogue. Do you feel validated?

Soros: Frankly, I do. For a long time, I did not have much self-confidence when it came to my conceptual framework. I often thought it was nothing but a personal obsession of mine, not necessarily of interest to other people. But that changed after the crash of 2008. For instance Mervyn King, governor of the Bank of England, admitted that there was more to my ideas than he had believed. I found that rather satisfying. Needless to say, he went up in my estimation.

SCHMITZ: When I discussed this book project with friends, many asked why you are devoting a lot of time to a book on the arcane and complicated details of the euro crisis, even though you could be just enjoying your retirement. You are eighty-three and a newlywed.

SOROS: I try to live life as fully as possible, and having a good time is not my idea of having a good time. You might call me a history junkie because I really do want to influence history. I have always harbored an exaggerated view of my self-importance. I wanted to be an economic reformer, like Keynes, or even better, a scientist like Einstein.

SCHMITZ: Comparing yourself to these figures is a tall order. In comparison, are you happy with your achievements?

SOROS: The truth is that my reputation is based not on my philosophical or philanthropic achievements but on my success in making money. I am aware of that. But I like my persona. It is my creation and I am proud of it. That is a big change from the way I used to feel during the most productive period of my business career. For some reason, I used to be ashamed of myself, and I have simply grown out of that. I also used to be very isolated, and now I am very involved. So when all is said and done, being a public person has made me a happier private person.

APPENDIX

Fallibility, Reflexivity, and the Human Uncertainty Principle

These conversations about markets, the euro crisis, and other matters are all informed by George Soros's theory of reflexivity, which he began developing as a student at the London School of Economics in the early 1950s. It has preoccupied him ever since. In January 2014 the *Journal of Economic Methodology* dedicated a special issue to reflexivity. George Soros's contribution to that issue is reprinted here by permission of Taylor & Francis Ltd, www.tandfonline.com. It is the clearest and most precise statement available of the philosophical theory that has informed his career as an investor and philanthropist.

1. INTRODUCTION

Of course I did not discover reflexivity. Earlier observers recognized it, or at least aspects of it, often under a different name. Frank H. Knight (1921) explored the difference between risk and uncertainty. John Maynard Keynes (1936, chap. 12) compared financial markets to a beauty contest where the participants had to guess who would be the most popular choice. The sociologist Robert King Merton (1949) wrote about self-fulfilling prophecies, unintended consequences, and the bandwagon effect. Karl Popper spoke of the "Oedipus effect" in *The Poverty of Historicism* (1957, chap. 5).

My own conceptual framework has its origins in my time as a student at the London School of Economics in the late 1950s. I took my final exams one year early, so I had a year to fill before I was qualified to receive my degree. I could choose my tutor, and I chose Karl Popper, whose book *The Open Society and Its Enemies* (1945) had made a profound impression on me.

In Popper's other great work, *Logik der Forschung* (1935), which was published in English as *The Logic of Scientific Discovery* (1959), he argued that the empirical truth cannot be known with absolute certainty. Even scientific laws cannot be verified beyond a shadow of a doubt: they can only be falsified by testing. One failed test is enough to falsify, but no amount of conforming instances is sufficient to verify. Scientific laws are always hypothetical in character, and their validity remains open to falsification.

While I was reading Popper I was also studying economic theory, and I was struck by the contradiction between Popper's emphasis on imperfect understanding and the theory of perfect competition in economics, which postulated perfect knowledge. This led me to start questioning the assumptions of economic theory. I replaced the postulates of rational expectations and efficient markets with my own principles of fallibility and reflexivity.

After college I started working in the financial markets,

where I had not much use for the economic theories I had studied in college. Strangely enough, the conceptual framework I had developed under Popper's influence provided me with much more valuable insights. And while I was engaged in making money, I did not lose my interest in philosophy.

I published my first book, *The Alchemy of Finance*, in 1987. In that book I tried to explain the philosophical underpinnings of my approach to financial markets. The book attracted a certain amount of attention. It has been read by many people in the hedge-fund industry, and it is taught in business schools. But the philosophical arguments in that book and subsequent books (Soros 1998, 2000) did not make much of an impression on the economics departments of universities. My framework was largely dismissed as the conceit of a man who has been successful in business and therefore fancies himself as a philosopher. With my theories largely ignored by academia, I began to regard myself as a failed philosopher—I even gave a lecture entitled, "A Failed Philosopher Tries Again."

All that changed as a result of the financial crisis of 2008. My understanding of reflexivity enabled me both to anticipate the crisis and to deal with it when it finally struck (Soros 2008, 2009). When the fallout of the crisis spread from the United States to Europe and around the world, it enabled me to explain and predict events better than most others (Soros 2012). The crisis put in stark relief the failings of orthodox economic theory (Soros 2010). As people have realized how badly traditional economics has failed, interest in reflexivity has grown.

Economics is in a period of intellectual flux, and though

some economists will cling to ideas of market efficiency and rationality to their final days, many others are eager to pursue alternative approaches.

In this essay I will articulate my current thinking. In Section 2, I shall explain the concepts of fallibility and reflexivity in general terms. In Section 3, I will discuss the implications of my conceptual framework for the social sciences in general and for economics in particular. In Section 4, I will describe how my conceptual framework applies to the financial markets, with special mention of financial bubbles and the ongoing euro crisis. I will then conclude with some thoughts on the need for a new paradigm in social science.

2. FALLIBILITY AND REFLEXIVITY

I have a peculiar problem in explicating my conceptual framework. The framework deals with the relationship between thinking and reality, but the participants' thinking is part of the reality that they have to think about; that makes the relationship circular. Circles have no beginning or end, so I have to plunge in at an arbitrary point. That makes my ideas less clear when I put them into words than they are in my own mind. I am not the only one affected by this difficulty, but I feel obliged to warn the reader that this section will be more convoluted and less elegant than it ought to be; the rest of the paper is not affected.

My conceptual framework is built on two relatively simple propositions. The first is that in situations that have thinking participants, the participants' view of the world never perfectly corresponds to the actual state of affairs. People can gain knowledge of individual facts, but when it comes to formulating theories or forming an overall view, their perspective is bound to be either biased or inconsistent, or both. That is the *principle of fallibility*.

The second proposition is that these imperfect views can influence the situation to which they relate through the actions of the participants. For example, if investors believe that markets are efficient, then that belief will change the way they invest, and that in turn will change the nature of the markets in which they are participating (though not necessarily making them more efficient). That is the *principle of reflexivity*.

The two principles are tied together like Siamese twins, but fallibility is the firstborn: without fallibility, there would be no reflexivity. Both principles can be observed operating in the real world. So when my critics say that I am merely stating the obvious, they are right—but only up to a point. What makes my propositions interesting is that they contradict some of the basic tenets of economic theory. My conceptual framework deserves attention not because it constitutes a new discovery, but because something as commonsensical as reflexivity has been so studiously ignored by economists. The field of economics has gone to great lengths to eliminate the uncertainty associated with reflexivity in order to formulate universally valid laws similar to Newtonian physics. In doing so, economists set themselves an impossible task. The uncertainty associated with fallibility and reflexivity is inherent in the human condition. To make this point, I lump together the two concepts as the *human uncertainty principle*.

Fallibility

The complexity of the world in which we live exceeds our capacity to comprehend it. Confronted by a reality of extreme complexity, we are obliged to resort to various methods of simplification: generalizations, dichotomies, metaphors, decision rules, and moral precepts, just to mention a few. These mental constructs take on a (subjective) existence of their own, further complicating the situation.

The structure of the brain is another source of fallibility. Recent advances in brain science have begun to provide some insight into how the brain functions, and they have substantiated David Hume's insight that reason is the slave of passion. The idea of a disembodied intellect or reason is a figment of our imagination. The brain is bombarded by millions of sensory impulses, but consciousness can process only seven or eight subjects concurrently. The impulses need to be condensed, ordered, and interpreted under immense time pressure; mistakes and distortions can't be avoided. Brain science adds many new insights to my contention that our understanding of the world in which we live is inherently imperfect.

Fallibility pervades our attempts to understand both natural and social phenomena, but it is not fallibility that distinguishes the social from the physical sciences. Rather, as will be discussed further in Section 3, the distinction comes from the fact that in social systems, fallible human beings are not merely scientific observers but also active participants in the system themselves. That is what makes social systems reflexive.

Reflexivity

The concept of reflexivity needs some further explication. It applies exclusively to situations that have thinking participants. The participants' thinking serves two functions. One is to understand the world in which we live; I call this the *cognitive function*. The other is to make an impact on the world and to advance the participants' interests; I call this the *manipulative function*. I use the term "manipulative" to emphasize intentionality.

The two functions connect the participants' thinking (subjective reality) and the actual state of affairs (objective reality) in opposite directions. In the cognitive function, the participant is cast in the role of a passive observer: the direction of causation is from the world to the mind. In the manipulative function, the participants play an active role: the direction of causation is from the mind to the world. Both functions are subject to fallibility.

When both the cognitive and manipulative functions operate at the same time, they may interfere with each other. How? By depriving each function of the independent variable that would be needed to determine the value of the dependent variable. The independent variable of one function is the dependent variable of the other; thus neither function has a *genuinely independent variable*—the relationship is circular or recursive. It is like a partnership in which each partner's view of the other influences his or her own behavior, and vice versa.

Lack of an Independent Criterion of Truth

If the cognitive function operated in isolation, without any interference from the manipulative function, it could produce knowledge. Knowledge is represented by true statements. A statement is true if it corresponds to the facts—that is what the correspondence theory of truth tells us. But if there is interference from the manipulative function, the facts no longer serve as an independent criterion because the statement may be the product of the manipulative function.

Consider the statement "It is raining." That statement is true or false depending on whether it is, in fact, raining. And whether people believe it is raining or not cannot change the facts. The agent can assess the statement without any interference from the manipulative function and thus gain knowledge.

Now consider the statement "I love you." The statement is reflexive. It will have an effect on the object of the affections of the person making the statement, and the recipient's response may then affect the feelings of the person making the statement, changing the truth-value of his or her original statement.

Self-Reference

Reflexivity has some affinity with the Liar's Paradox, which is a self-referential statement. "This sentence is false" is paradoxical. If the sentence is true, it means it is false, but if it is false, it means it is true. Bertrand Russell resolved the paradox by putting self-referential statements into a separate category and declaring them to be meaningless.

Following Russell, an important school of philosophy, logical positivism, banned self-referential statements. Ludwig Wittgenstein carried this program to its logical conclusion in his *Tractatus Logico-Philosophicus*, and in the end he concluded that he had embarked on an impossible task. In practice it is impossible to avoid either self-referential or reflexive statements. Consequently, the cognitive function can't produce all the knowledge that agents need to make decisions; they have to act on the basis of imperfect understanding. Although the manipulative function can make an impact on the world, outcomes are unlikely to correspond to expectations. There is bound to be some slippage between intentions and actions, and further slippage between actions and outcomes. Because agents base their decisions on inadequate knowledge, their actions are liable to have unintended consequences. This means that reflexivity introduces an element of uncertainty into both the agents' view of the world and into the world in which they participate.

Self-reference has been extensively analyzed by the Vienna school with which Popper was associated, but reflexivity has received much less attention. This is strange because reflexivity has an impact on the real world, whereas self-reference is confined to the universe of statements. In the real world, the participants' thinking finds expression not only in statements but also, of course, in various forms of action and behavior. That makes reflexivity a much broader phenomenon than self-reference: it connects the universe of thoughts with the universe of events. Bertrand Russell analyzed the Liar's Paradox in a timeless fashion. But reflexive systems are dynamic and unfold over time as the cognitive and manipulative functions perpetually chase each other. Once time is introduced, reflexivity creates indeterminacy and uncertainty rather than paradox.

Reflexive feedback loops between the cognitive and manipulative functions connect the realms of beliefs and events. The participants' views influence but do not determine the course of events, and the course of events influences but does not determine the participants' views. The influence is continuous and circular; that is what turns it into a feedback loop. As both the cognitive and manipulative functions are subject to fallibility, uncertainty is introduced into both the realms of beliefs and events. The process may be initiated from either direction, from a change in views, or from a change in circumstances.

Objective and Subjective Aspects of Reality

Reflexive feedback loops have *not* been rigorously analyzed, and when I originally encountered them and tried to study them, I ran into various difficulties. The main source of the trouble was that thinking is part of reality and the relationship of a part to the whole is very difficult to describe. The fact that thinking is not directly observable adds further complications; consequently, the definition of reflexivity will be much more complicated than the concept itself. The idea is that there is a two-way feedback loop connecting thinking and reality. The main feedback is between the participants' views and the actual course of events. But what about a direct two-way interaction between the various participants' views? And what about a solitary individual asking herself who she is and what she stands for and changing her behavior as a result of her own internal reflections?

To resolve these difficulties I propose distinguishing between the *objective* and *subjective* aspects of reality. Thinking constitutes the subjective aspect. It takes place in the privacy of the participants' minds and is not directly observable; only its material manifestations are. The objective aspect consists of observable events. In other words, the subjective aspect covers the participants' thinking and the objective aspect denotes all observable facts, whether in the outside world or inside the brain.

Free Will Versus Determinism

There is only one objective reality, but there are as many different subjective views as there are thinking participants. The views can be divided into different groups such as doubters and believers, trend followers and contrarians, Cartesians and empiricists—but these are simplifications and the categories are not fixed. Agents may hold views that are not easily categorized; moreover, they are free to choose between categories and they are free to switch. This is what is usually meant by free will, but I consider free will a misnomer. People's views are greatly influenced but not determined by external factors such as the views of others, heredity, upbringing, and prior experiences. So reality is halfway between free will and determinism.

Reflexivity can connect any two or more aspects of reality, setting up two-way feedback loops between them. We may then distinguish between two kinds of reflexivity: reflexive *relations*, like marriage or politics, which connect the subjective aspects of reality; and reflexive *events*, like the fiscal cliff or the euro crisis, which connect the subjective and objective

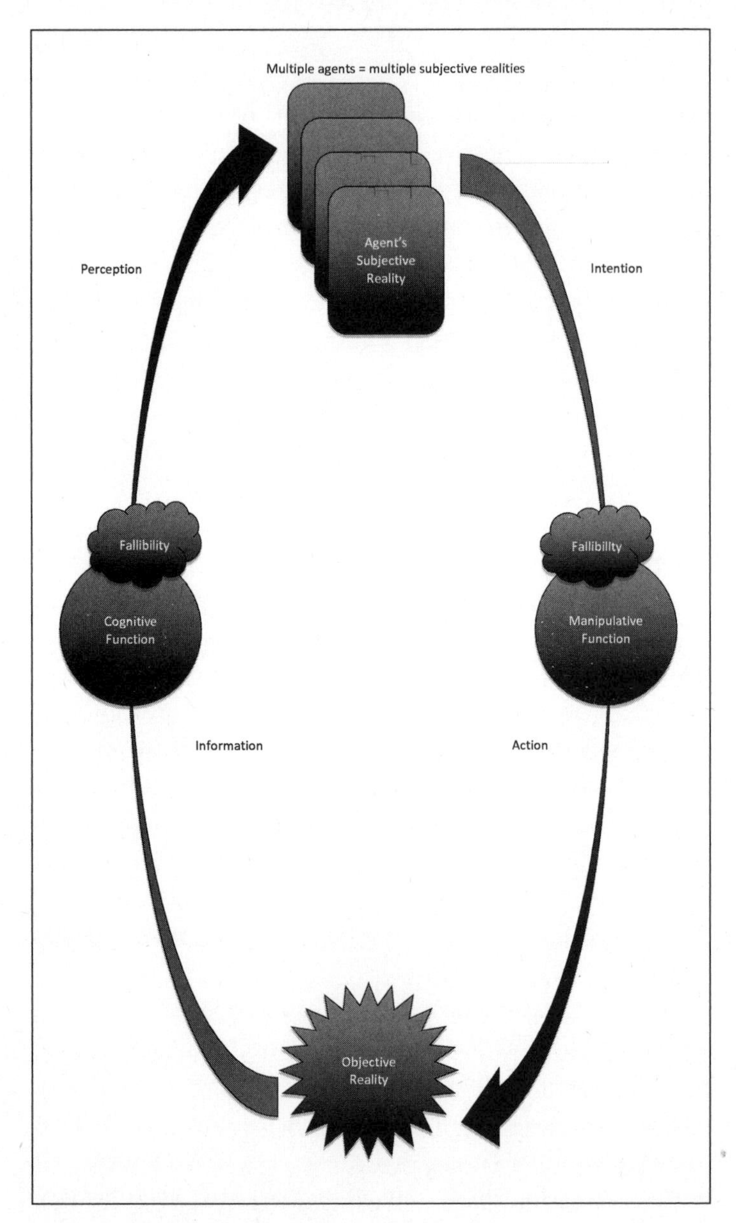

Figure 1. A Reflexive System.

aspects. In exceptional cases reflexivity may even occur within a single subjective aspect of reality, as in the case of a solitary individual reflecting on his own identity. This may be described as *self-reflexivity*.

When reality has no subjective aspect, there can be no reflexivity. In other words, the presence or absence of reflexivity serves as a criterion of demarcation between social and natural phenomena—a point I will discuss in detail in the next section.

Let me illustrate the difficulties in analyzing the relationship between thinking and reality with the help of a diagram. Figure 1 describes the roles of the cognitive and manipulative functions, fallibility, and intentionality. Together this might be thought of as a *reflexive system*.

I have indicated the presence of multiple participants, and therefore multiple subjective realities. Nevertheless, the diagram is inadequate because it would require three dimensions to show the multiple participants interacting with each other as well as with the objective aspect of reality.

The Human Uncertainty Principle

Frank H. Knight (1921) introduced an important distinction between risk and uncertainty. Risk occurs when there are multiple possible future states and the probabilities of those different future states occurring are known. Risk is well described by the laws of probability and statistics. Knightian uncertainty occurs when the probabilities of future states, or even the nature of possible future states, are not known.

At this point we need to recognize that it is fallibility that is the source of Knightian uncertainty in human affairs. Yes, reflexivity does introduce an element of uncertainty into both the participants' views and the actual course of events, but there are also other forms of fallibility that have the same effect. For instance, different participants have different goals, some of which may be in conflict with each other. Moreover, as Isaiah Berlin pointed out, each participant may be guided by a multiplicity of values that may not be self-consistent. The uncertainties created by these factors are more extensive than those specifically associated with reflexivity.

We must also remember that not all forms of fallibility create Knightian uncertainty. Some forms are subject to statistical analysis—human errors leading to road accidents, for example, or the many biases and errors discovered by behavioral economists. Other aspects of fallibility qualify as Knightian uncertainty—for example, probability analysis is not much help in understanding the misconceptions at the heart of the euro crisis.

Humans face quantifiable risks as well as Knightian uncertainty. There are many activities that are predictable, or at least their probabilities can be calculated. Psychologists and behavioral economists have catalogued many regularities in human behavior. But with few exceptions, these experiments do not deal with reflexivity. Most behavioral experiments assess people's perception of objective reality (e.g., trying to remember numbers, guess probabilities of different events, etc.) and thus are really measures of the fallibility of the cognitive function. The manipulative function is rarely studied. Thus, there is both uncertainty and regularity in human affairs. Reflexivity is only one source of uncertainty, albeit a powerful one.

Earlier I referred to the combination of reflexivity and fallibility as the *human uncertainty principle*. That makes it a broader concept than reflexivity. The human uncertainty principle is much more specific and stringent than the subjective skepticism that pervades Cartesian philosophy. It gives us objective reasons to believe that the theories held by the participants, as distinct from statements of specific facts, are liable to be biased or incomplete, or both.

3. PHILOSOPHY OF SOCIAL SCIENCE

The idea that the sciences should be unified goes back to the pre-Socratic Greeks and has been a subject of debate in philosophy ever since. Karl Popper (1935/1959, 1957) argued that science could be demarcated from metaphysics by his notion of falsifiable hypotheses; moreover, that falsifiable hypotheses could also provide methodological unity to the sciences.

Although I have drawn much inspiration from Popper, this is an important point where I differ from my mentor. I believe that reflexivity provides a strong challenge to the idea that natural and social science can be unified. I believe that social science can still be a valuable human endeavor, but in order for it to be so, we must recognize its fundamental differences from natural science.

Popper's Theory of Scientific Method

I base my argument on Popper's (1935/1959) theory of scientific method. Let me start by summarizing his beautifully simple and elegant scheme. It consists of three elements and three operations. The three elements are scientific laws of universal and timeless validity and two sets of singular conditions that Popper calls the cause and the effect. The three operations are prediction, explanation, and testing. When a scientific law is combined with the cause, it provides predictions. When a scientific law is combined with the effect, it provides explanations. In this sense, predictions and explanations are symmetrical and reversible through the logic of deduction. That leaves testing.

On this last point Popper had a key insight. According to Popper, scientific laws are hypothetical in character; they cannot be verified, but they can be falsified by empirical testing. The key to the success of scientific method is that it can test generalizations of universal validity with the help of singular observations. One failed test is sufficient to falsify a theory, but no amount of confirming instances is sufficient to verify it. Generalizations that cannot be tested do not qualify as scientific.

This is a brilliant construct that makes science both empirical and rational. According to Popper, it is empirical because we *test* our theories by observing whether the predictions we derive from them are true, and it is rational because we use deductive logic in doing so. Popper dispenses with inductive logic, which he considers invalid, and he gives testing a central role instead. He also makes a strong case for critical thinking by asserting that scientific laws are only provisionally valid and remain open to reexamination. The three salient features of Popper's scheme are the symmetry between prediction and explanation, the asymmetry between verification and falsification, and the central role of testing. These three features allow science to grow, improve, and innovate.

Problems of Social Science

Popper's scheme has worked extraordinarily well for the study of natural phenomena, but the human uncertainty principle throws a monkey wrench into the supreme simplicity and elegance of Popper's scheme. The symmetry between prediction and explanation is destroyed because the future is genuinely uncertain, and therefore cannot be predicted with the same degree of certainty as it can be explained in retrospect. One might object that uncertainty exists in all realms of science. But whereas Werner Heisenberg's uncertainty principle in quantum mechanics is subject to the laws of probability and statistics, the deep Knightian uncertainties of human affairs associated with the human uncertainty principle are not.

Even more important, the central role of testing is endangered. Should the initial and final conditions include or exclude the participant's thinking? The question is important because testing requires replicating those conditions. If the participants' thinking is included, it is difficult to determine what the initial and final conditions are because the participants' views can only be inferred from their statements or actions. If the participants' thinking is excluded, the initial and final conditions do not constitute singular observations because the same objective conditions may be associated with very different subjective views. In either case, testing cannot meet the requirements of Popper's scheme. This limitation does not preclude social sciences from producing worthwhile generalizations, but they are unlikely to match the predictive power of the laws of physics. Empirical testing ought to play a central role in social science as well, but it should not be expected to produce universal and timeless generalizations with symmetrical and reversible explanatory and predictive powers. This point will be elaborated at the end of Section 4.

The Structure of Events

I contend that situations that have thinking participants have a different structure from natural phenomena. The difference lies in the role thinking plays. In natural phenomena, thinking plays no *causal* role. Events unfold irrespective of the views held by the observers. The structure of natural events can be described as a chain of cause and effect generating a stream of objective facts, without any interference from the subjective aspects of reality (see Figure 2).

In natural science, the outside observer is engaged only in the cognitive function, and the facts provide a reliable criterion by which the truth of the observers' theories can be judged. So the outside observer can obtain knowledge about the natural phenomena she is observing. Based on that

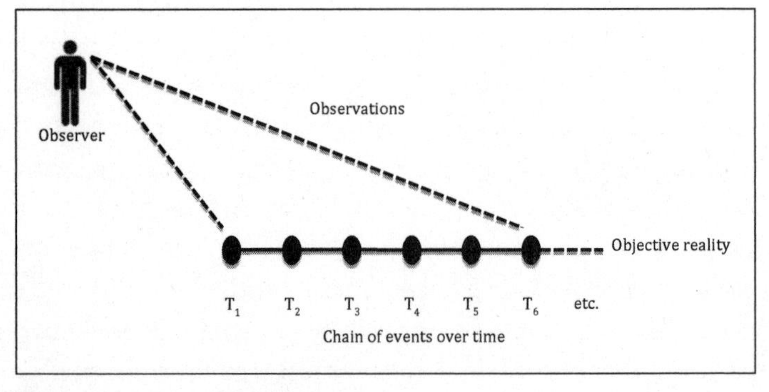

Figure 2. Natural Phenomena

knowledge, nature can be successfully manipulated. That manipulation may change the state of the physical world, but it does not change the laws that govern that world. We can use our understanding of the physical world to create airplanes, but the invention of the airplane did not change the laws of aerodynamics.

By contrast, in human affairs, thinking is *part of* the subject matter. The course of events leads not only from facts to facts but also from facts to the participants' perceptions (the cognitive function) and from the participants' decisions to facts (the manipulative function).

Figure 3 is a simplified presentation of the structure of social events. It illustrates that there is only one objective aspect but as many subjective aspects of reality as there are thinking participants. The reflexive feedback loops between the objective and subjective aspects of reality create a lace-like pattern, which is superimposed on the direct line leading

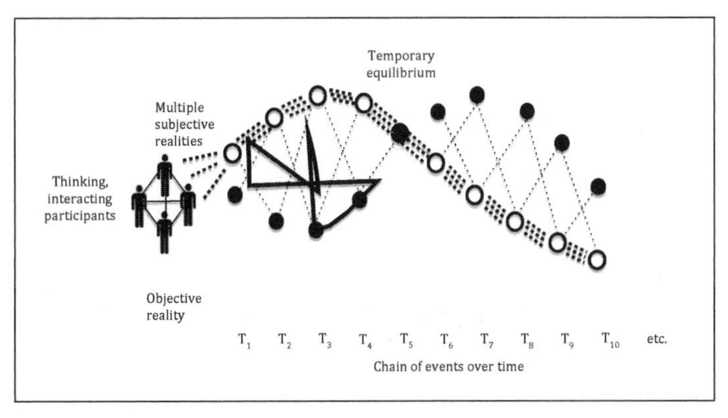

Figure 3. Social Phenomena

from one set of facts to the next and deflects it from what it would be if there were no feedback loops. The feedback sometimes brings the subjective and objective aspects closer together and sometimes drives them further apart. The two aspects are aligned, but only loosely—the human uncertainty principle implies that a perfect alignment is the exception rather than the rule.

Physics Envy

Popper's scheme would require social scientists to produce generalizations of universal and timeless validity that determine the alignment of the objective and subjective aspects of reality. If the human uncertainty principle is valid, that is an impossible task. Yet the achievements of natural science, exemplified by Newtonian physics, were so alluring that economists and other social scientists have tried incredibly hard to establish such generalizations. They suffered from what I like to call "physics envy." In order to achieve the impossible, they invented or postulated some kind of fixed relationship between the participants' thinking and the actual course of events. Karl Marx asserted that the material conditions of production determined the ideological superstructure; Sigmund Freud maintained that people's behavior was determined by the unconscious. Both claimed scientific status for their theories, but Popper rightly argued that their theories could not be falsified by testing.

However, Popper did not go far enough. The same argument applies to the mainstream economic theory currently taught in universities. It is an axiomatic system based on deductive logic, not empirical evidence. If the axioms are true, so are the mathematical deductions. In this regard, economic theory resembles Euclidian geometry. But Euclid's postulates are modeled on conditions prevailing in the real world, whereas at least some of the postulates of economics, notably rational choice and rational expectations, are dictated by the desire to imitate Newtonian physics rather than real-world evidence.

This ill-fated attempt by economists to slavishly imitate physics has a long history. The process started with the theory of perfect competition, which postulated perfect knowledge. That postulate was later modified to universally available perfect information. When that postulate proved inadequate, Lionel Robbins, who was my professor at the London School of Economics, defined the task of economics as the allocation of limited means to unlimited alternative ends (Robbins 1932). He specifically excluded the study of the means and the ends themselves. By taking the prevailing values and methods of production as given, he eliminated reflexivity as a possible subject of study for economics. Subsequently, this approach reached its apex with the rational expectations and efficient market hypotheses in the 1960s and 1970s.

To be sure, physics envy is not unjustified. The achievements of natural science stand as convincing testimony to man's ability to use reason. Unfortunately, these achievements do not ensure that human behavior is always governed by reason.

Human Uncertainty as an Impediment to Scientific Method

The human uncertainty principle not only prevents the social sciences from producing results comparable to physics; it interferes with scientific method in other ways as well. I shall mention only one of them.

As we have seen, natural phenomena provide a genuinely independent criterion for judging the validity of generalizations, but the facts produced by social processes do not do so because they are influenced by theories held by participants. This makes social theories themselves subject to reflexivity. In other words, they serve not only a cognitive but also a manipulative function.

To be sure, the generalizations and observations of natural scientists are also theory laden, and they influence the selection of facts, but they do not influence the facts themselves. Heisenberg's uncertainty principle showed that the act of observation impacts a quantum system. But the discovery of the uncertainty principle itself did not alter the behavior of quantum particles one iota. The principle applied before Heisenberg discovered it and will continue to apply long after human observers are gone. But social theories—whether Marxism, market fundamentalism, or the theory of reflexivity—can affect the subject matter to which they refer.

Scientific method is supposed to be devoted to the pursuit of truth. But why should social science confine itself to passively studying social phenomena when it can be used to actively change the state of affairs? The temptation to use scientific theories to change reality rather than to understand it is much greater than in natural science. Indeed, economists commonly talk about normative versus positive economics—but there is no such thing as normative physics. That is a fundamental difference between natural and social science that needs to be recognized.

A Spectrum Between Physical and Social Sciences

In my argument I have drawn a sharp distinction between the social and natural sciences. But such dichotomies are usually not found in reality; rather, we introduce them in our efforts to make some sense out of an otherwise confusing reality. Indeed, though the dichotomy between physics and the social sciences seems clear-cut, there are other sciences, such as biology and the study of animal societies, that occupy intermediate positions.

The distinction I have drawn between natural and social science consists of the presence or absence of thinking participants who have a will of their own. That begs the question of what constitutes a "thinking participant." One might reasonably ask whether a chimpanzee, a dolphin, or a computerized stock-trading program is a thinking participant. In some fields, superior data-crunching capacity may trump the human imagination, as the chess contest between Big Blue and Gary Kasparov has shown. And automatic trading systems appear to be currently outperforming hedge funds run by humans. However, I would note that humans have some unique characteristics, notably language, emotions, and culture. Both our individual and shared subjective reality is far richer and more complex than any other creature or man-made invention.

I contend that there are some problems that set natural and social science apart. I have focused on one such fundamental problem area. It presents itself both in the subject matter and its scientific study, so that it may be conveniently treated as two closely interrelated problems. Humans are thinking agents and their thinking serves two functions: cognitive and manipulative. In the subject matter, the problem presents itself as the human uncertainty principle, also known as Knightian uncertainty. That has no equivalent in natural science. For scientific method, the problem is more complicated because scientists are also human beings and their thinking also serves two functions. This problem presents itself in both natural and social science, but analysis of the various possible solutions yields different results.

Science is a discipline that seeks to perfect the cognitive function by artificially isolating itself from the manipulative function. It does so by submitting itself to a number of conventions such as insisting on empirical tests that can be replicated and/or observed by others. Popper's scheme shows what natural science can achieve by obeying those rules and conventions. As I have shown, the human uncertainty principle prevents social science from matching these achievements. But there is also a flip side to be considered: What happens when those rules and conventions are not observed? Remember that my criterion of demarcation between natural and social science is that the latter is reflexive, the former is not. In other words, social science can change objective reality by influencing the participants' views, but natural science cannot because its subject matter has no thinking participants. That is what I meant when I remarked in *The Alchemy of Finance* that the alchemists made a mistake in trying to change the nature of base metals by incantation. Instead, they should have focused their attention on the financial markets, where they could have succeeded. Now I need to take my analysis further.

Natural science can work wonders as long as it follows Popper's scheme because it has a purely objective criterion, namely, the facts, by which the truth or validity of its laws can be judged; but it cannot produce anything worthwhile by cheating on the testing process. Cars that do not obey the laws of physics will not move, airplanes will not fly.

How about social science? We have seen that Popper's scheme cannot be expected to produce comparable results. On the other hand, social theories also serve a manipulative function, and their influence on objective reality may prove quite satisfactory from the point of view of their proponents—at least for a while, until objective reality reasserts itself and the outcome fails to correspond to expectations. There are many statements that fit this pattern. President Obama managed to make the post-2008 recession shorter and shallower by asserting that the economy was fundamentally sound and promising a speedy recovery, but he paid a heavy political price when reality failed to live up to his promises. Fed chairman Alan Greenspan operated much the same way, but his Delphic utterances were more difficult to prove wrong. Both Freud and Marx sought to gain acceptance for their theories by claiming scientific status. One of the most interesting cases is the efficient markets hypothesis and its political companion, market fundamentalism. We shall see that the mechanism that provides some degree of justification for the claim that markets are always right is reflexivity, not rational expectations. Yet a false explanation can be subjectively more appealing than what I consider to be the true one. The efficient market hypothesis allows economic theory to lay claim to the status of a hard science like physics. And market fundamentalism allows the financially successful to claim that they are serving the public interest by pursing their self-interest. That is a powerful combination that dominated the field until it caused a lot of damage in the financial crisis of 2007–2008. Surprisingly, it survived that debacle: the conservative wing of the Republican Party managed to pin the blame for the financial crisis on the government rather than the private sector. To correct this fateful mistake, I will propose a methodological convention.

A Methodological Convention

I propose renouncing Popper's doctrine of the unity of science and recognizing a fundamental difference between natural and social phenomena—not as an empirical truth but as a methodological convention. The convention asserts that social science cannot be expected to produce results comparable to physics by using the same methods; however, it sets no limits on what social science may be able to accomplish by employing different methods. The convention will protect scientific method by preventing the social sciences from parading with borrowed feathers. It should not be taken, however, as a demotion or devaluation of social science. On the contrary, it should open up new vistas by liberating social science from the slavish imitation of natural science and protecting it from being judged by the wrong standards.

The Limits and Promise of Social Science

Interestingly, both Karl Popper and Friedrich Hayek recognized in their famous exchange in the pages of *Economica* (Popper 1944) that the social sciences cannot produce results comparable to physics. Hayek inveighed against the mechanical and uncritical application of the quantitative methods of natural science. He called it "scientism." And Popper wrote *The Poverty of Historicism* (1957), in which he argued that history is not determined by universally valid scientific laws. Nevertheless, Popper proclaimed what he called the "doctrine of the unity of method," by which he meant that both the natural and the social sciences should use the same methods and be judged by the same criteria.

By proclaiming the doctrine, Popper sought to distinguish pseudo-scientific theories like those of Marx and Freud from mainstream economics. As mentioned before, Popper did not go far enough: rational choice theory and the efficient market hypothesis are just as pseudo-scientific as Marxist and Freudian theories.

As I see it, the implication of the human uncertainty principle is that the subject matter of the natural and the social sciences is fundamentally different; therefore, they need to develop different methods and should be held to different standards. Economic theory should not be expected to meet the standards established by Newtonian physics. In fact, if it did produce universally valid laws, as Frank Knight (1921, 28) pointed out, economic profit itself would be impossible:

> If all changes were to take place in accordance with invariable and universally known laws, [so that] they could be

> foreseen for an indefinite period in advance of their occurrence, . . . profit or loss would not arise.

I contend that Popper's scheme cannot produce results in the human sphere comparable to the amazing achievement of physics. The slavish imitation of natural science can easily produce misleading results, sometimes with disastrous consequences.

A methodological convention that merely asserts that the social sciences should not be confined to the same methods and be judged by the same criteria as the natural sciences may not seem like an adequate remedy for the ills I have identified. But look at the straitjacket Lionel Robbins imposed on economics: it prevented economists from recognizing reflexivity and encouraged the development of synthetic financial instruments and risk management techniques that ignore Knightian uncertainty, with disastrous consequences from which we have not yet found an escape.

I admit that the proposed methodological convention is only a starting point, and it begs the question of what social scientists *should* do, what methods they should use, and by what criteria they should be judged. Others writing in *the Journal of Economic Methodology* may have specific answers; I have only a partial one. Any valid methodology of social science must explicitly recognize both fallibility and reflexivity and the Knightian uncertainty they create. Empirical testing ought to remain a decisive criterion for judging whether a theory qualifies as scientific, but in light of the human uncertainty principle in social systems, it cannot always be as rigorous as Popper's scheme requires. Nor can universally and timelessly valid theories be expected to yield determinate predictions, because future events are contingent on future decisions, which are based on imperfect knowledge. Time and context-bound generalizations may yield more specific explanations and predictions than timeless and universal ones.[1]

4. FINANCIAL MARKETS

Financial markets provide an excellent laboratory for testing the ideas I have put forward in the previous sections. The course of events is easier to observe than in most other areas. Many of the facts take a quantitative form, and the data are well recorded and well preserved. The opportunity for testing occurs because my interpretation of financial markets directly contradicts the efficient market hypothesis, which has been the prevailing paradigm.

The efficient market hypothesis claims that markets tend toward equilibrium; that deviations occur in a random fashion and can be attributed to exogenous shocks. It is then a testable proposition whether the efficient market hypothesis

1. Postscript: When I wrote this article I was troubled by drawing an overly sharp distinction between the natural and the social sciences. Eric Beinhocker's (2013) article in this symposium and a workshop at the Central European University on October 8, 2013, led me to modify my views on separating the two. I still think that the methodological convention I proposed is needed in the near term in order to break the stranglehold of rational choice theory, but I realize it could do more harm than good in the long term. As I stated above, there is a spectrum between the physical and the social sciences. Beinhocker is right in arguing that we should study the spectrum rather than attributing reflexivity exclusively to the domain of the social sciences. There are many similarities between human and nonhuman complex systems, which could be obfuscated by the proposed convention. Instead of denying the unity of science, we ought to redefine scientific method so that it is not confined to Popper's model.

or my theory of reflexivity is better at explaining and predicting events. I contend that my theory of reflexivity is superior, even in its current rudimentary stage of development for explaining and predicting financial markets in general, and historical events like the financial crisis of 2007–2008 and the subsequent euro crisis in particular.

My Conceptual Framework

Let me state the three key concepts of my approach—fallibility, reflexivity, and the human uncertainty principle—as they apply to the financial markets. First, fallibility. Market prices of financial assets do not accurately reflect their fundamental value because they do not even aim to do so. Prices reflect market participants' expectations of future market prices. Moreover, market participants are subject to fallibility; consequently, their expectations about the discounted present value of future earnings flows are likely to diverge from reality. The divergence may range from the negligible to the significant. This is in direct contradiction to the efficient market hypothesis, which does not admit fallibility.

Second, reflexivity. Instead of playing a purely passive role in reflecting an underlying reality, financial markets also have an active role: they can *affect* the future earnings flows they are supposed to reflect. That is the point that behavioral economists have missed. Behavioral economics focuses on only half of the reflexive process: cognitive fallibility leading to the mispricing of assets; they do not concern themselves with the effects that mispricing can have on the fundamentals.

There are various pathways by which the mispricing of

financial assets can affect the so-called fundamentals. The most widely used are those that involve the use of leverage—both debt and equity leveraging. For instance, companies can improve their earnings per share by issuing shares at inflated prices—at least for a while. Markets may give the impression that they are always right, but the mechanism at work is very different from the one implied by the prevailing paradigm.

Third, the human uncertainty principle turns what economic theory treats as timeless generalizations into a time-bound historical process. If agents act on the basis of their perfect understanding, equilibrium is far from a universally and timelessly prevailing condition of financial markets. Markets may just as easily tend away from a putative equilibrium as toward it. Instead of universally and timelessly prevailing, equilibrium becomes an extreme condition in which subjective market expectations correspond to objective reality. Theoretically, such a correspondence could be brought about by either the cognitive or the manipulative function by itself—either perceptions can change to match reality or perceptions can lead to actions that change reality to match perceptions. But in practice such a correspondence is more likely to be the product of a reflexive interaction between the two functions. Whereas economics views equilibrium as the normal, indeed necessary state of affairs, I view such periods of stability as exceptional. Rather, I focus on the reflexive feedback loops that characterize financial markets and cause them to be changing over time.

Negative Versus Positive Feedback Loops

Reflexive feedback loops can be either negative or positive. Negative feedback brings the participants' views and the actual situation closer together; positive feedback drives them further apart. In other words, a negative feedback process is self-correcting. It can go on forever, and if there are no significant changes in external reality, it may eventually lead to an equilibrium in which the participants' views come to correspond to the actual state of affairs.

That is what rational expectations theory expects to happen in financial markets. It postulates that there is a single correct set of expectations that people's views will converge around and that deviations are random—there are no systematic errors between participants' forecasts and what comes to pass. That postulate bears no resemblance to reality, but it is a core tenet of economics as it is currently taught in universities and even used in the models of central banks. In practice, market participants' expectations diverge from reality to a greater or lesser extent, and their errors may be correlated and significantly biased. That is the generic cause of price distortions. So equilibrium, which is the *central* case in mainstream economic theory, turns out to be an extreme case of negative feedback, a *limiting* case in my conceptual framework. Because equilibrium is so extreme that it is unlikely to prevail in reality, I prefer to speak of *near-equilibrium* conditions.

By contrast, a positive feedback process is self-reinforcing. It cannot go on forever because eventually the participants' views would become so far removed from objective reality that the participants would have to recognize them as unrealistic.

Nor can the iterative process occur without any change in the actual state of affairs, because positive feedback reinforces whatever tendency prevails in the real world. Instead of equilibrium, we are faced with a dynamic disequilibrium, or what may be described as *far-from-equilibrium* situations.

There are myriad feedback loops at work in financial markets at any point of time. Some of them are positive, others negative. As long as they are more or less in balance, they cancel each other out and market fluctuations do not have a definite direction. I compare these swings to the waves sloshing around in a swimming pool, as opposed to the tides and currents that may prevail when positive feedbacks preponderate. Because positive feedbacks are self-reinforcing, occasionally they may become so big that they overshadow all other happenings in the market.

Negative feedback loops tend to be more ubiquitous, but positive feedback loops are more interesting because they can cause big moves both in market prices and in the underlying fundamentals. A positive feedback process that runs its full course is initially self-reinforcing in one direction, but eventually it is liable to reach a climax or reversal point, after which it becomes self-reinforcing in the opposite direction. But positive feedback processes do not necessarily run their full course; they may be aborted at any time by negative feedback.

Boom-Bust Processes

Building on these ideas, I have developed a theory about boom-bust processes, or bubbles (Soros 1987, 2008). Every bubble has two components: an underlying trend that prevails

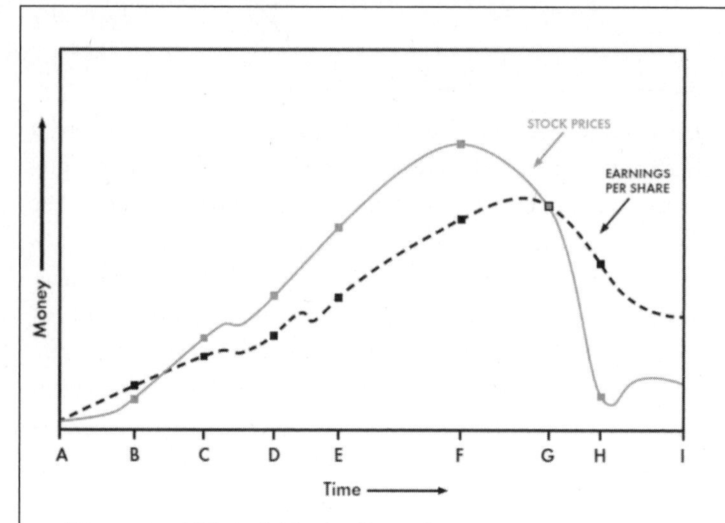

Figure 4. A Typical Market Boom-Bust

In the initial change (AB) a new positive earning trend is not yet recognized. Then comes a period of acceleration (BC) when the trend is recognized and reinforced by expectations. A period of testing may intervene when either earnings or expectations waiver (CD). If the positive trend and bias survive the testing, both emerge stronger. Conviction develops and is no longer shaken by a setback in earnings (DE). The gap between expectations and reality becomes wider (EF) until the moment of truth arrives when reality can no longer sustain the exaggerated expectations and the bias is recognized as such (F). A twilight period ensues when people continue to play the game although they no longer believe in it (FG). Eventually a crossover point (G) is reached when the trend turns down and prices lose their last prop. This leads to a catastrophic downward acceleration (GH) commonly known as the crash. The pessimism becomes overdone, earnings stabilize, and prices recover somewhat (HI).

in reality and a misconception relating to that trend (see Figure 4). A boom-bust process is set in motion when a trend and a misconception positively reinforce each other. The process is liable to be tested by negative feedback along the way, giving rise to climaxes that may or may not turn out to be genuine. If a trend is strong enough to survive the test, both the trend and the misconception will be further reinforced. Eventually, market expectations become so far removed from reality that people are forced to recognize that a misconception is involved. A twilight period ensues during which doubts grow and more people lose faith, but the prevailing trend is sustained by inertia. As Chuck Prince, former head of Citigroup said during the twilight of the "superbubble": "As long as the music is playing, you've got to get up and dance. We're still dancing." Eventually a point is reached when the trend is reversed; it then becomes self-reinforcing in the opposite direction. Boom-bust processes tend to be asymmetrical: booms are slow to develop and take a long time to become unsustainable; busts tend to be more abrupt, due to forced liquidation of unsustainable positions and the asymmetries introduced by leverage.

The simplest case is a real estate boom. The trend that precipitates it is easy credit; the misconception is that the value of the collateral is independent of the availability of credit. As a matter of fact, the relationship is reflexive. When credit becomes cheaper and more easily available, activity picks up and real estate values rise. There are fewer defaults, credit performance improves, and lending standards are relaxed. So at the height of the boom, the amount of credit involved is at its maximum and a reversal precipitates forced liquidation, depressing real estate values. Amazingly, the misconception continues to recur in various guises.

Other bubbles are based on different misconceptions. For instance, the international banking crisis of 1982 revolved around sovereign debt, in which case no collateral was involved. The creditworthiness of the sovereign borrowers was measured by various debt ratios, such as debt to GDP or debt service to exports. These ratios were considered objective criteria, but in fact they were reflexive. When the recycling of petrodollars in the 1970s increased the flow of credit to countries such as Brazil, their debt ratios improved, which encouraged further inflows and started a bubble. In 1980, Federal Reserve chairman Paul Volcker raised interest rates in the United States to arrest inflation, and the sovereign debt bubble burst in 1982.

Bubbles are not the only form in which reflexivity manifests itself. They are just the most dramatic and the most directly contradictory to the efficient market hypothesis, so they do deserve special attention. But reflexivity can take many other forms. In currency markets, for instance, the upside and downside are symmetrical, so there is no sign of an asymmetry between boom and bust. But there is no sign of equilibrium, either. Freely floating exchange rates tend to move in large, multiyear waves.

Markets Versus Regulators

One of the most important and interesting reflexive interactions takes place between the financial authorities and financial markets. Because markets do not tend toward equilibrium, they are prone to produce periodic crises. Financial crises lead to regulatory reforms. That is how central banking and the regulation of financial markets have evolved. Financial authorities and market participants alike act on the basis of imperfect understanding, and that makes the interaction between them reflexive.

Bubbles occur only intermittently, but the interplay between authorities and markets is an ongoing process. Misunderstandings by either side usually stay within reasonable bounds because market reactions provide useful feedback to the authorities, allowing them to correct their mistakes. But occasionally the mistakes prove to be self-validating, setting in motion vicious or virtuous circles. Such feedback loops resemble bubbles in the sense that they are initially self-reinforcing but eventually self-defeating. Indeed, the intervention of the authorities to deal with periodic financial crises played a crucial role in the development of a superbubble that burst in 2007–2008 (Soros 2008, 2009). The interplay between markets and regulators is also at the heart of the euro crisis.

The Euro Crisis

I have been following the euro crisis closely ever since its inception. I have written numerous articles that have been collected in a book (Soros 2012). It would be impossible to summarize all my arguments for this essay; therefore, I shall focus only on the reflexive interaction between markets and authorities. Both acted on the basis of their imperfect understanding.

The design of the common currency had many flaws. Some of them were known at the time the euro was introduced.

Everybody, for example, knew that it was an incomplete currency; it had a central bank, but it didn't have a common treasury. The crash of 2008, however, revealed many other deficiencies. In retrospect, the most important was that by transferring the right to print money to an independent central bank, member countries ran the risk of default on their government bonds. In a developed country with its own currency, the risk of default is absent because it can always print money. But by ceding or transferring that right to an independent central bank, which no member-state actually controls, the member-states put themselves in the position of Third World countries that borrow in a foreign currency.

This fact was not recognized either by the markets or by the authorities prior to the crash of 2008, testifying to their fallibility. When the euro was introduced, the authorities actually declared government bonds to be riskless. Commercial banks were not required to set aside any capital reserves against their holdings of government bonds. The European Central Bank accepted all government bonds on equal terms at the discount window. This set up a perverse incentive for commercial banks to buy the debt of the weaker governments in order to earn what eventually became just a few basis points, because interest rates on government bonds converged to practically zero. This convergence in interest rates caused divergences in economic performance. The weaker countries enjoyed real estate and consumption booms, while Germany, which was dealing with the burden of reunification, had to adopt fiscal austerity and structural reforms.

After the Lehman bankruptcy, European finance ministers declared that no other systemically important financial institution would be allowed to fail; Chancellor Merkel then insisted that the obligation should fall on each country individually, not on the European Union or the eurozone collectively. That was the onset of the euro crisis. It took markets more than a year to react to it. Only when Greece revealed a much larger than expected fiscal deficit did markets realize that Greece might actually default on its debt—and they raised risk premiums with a vengeance, not only on Greek bonds but on the bonds of all the heavily indebted member countries.

A Greek default would have created a worse banking crisis than the Lehman bankruptcy. The authorities put together a number of rescue packages, but they always did too little, too late, so conditions in Greece continued to deteriorate. This set a pattern for the other heavily indebted countries such as Spain, Italy, Portugal, and Ireland as well. Although the actions of the ECB have calmed the markets, the crisis is still far from resolved. Rather than an association of equals, the eurozone became divided into two classes: creditors and debtors. In a financial crisis, the creditors call the shots. The policies they are imposing perpetuate the division because the debtors have to pay risk premiums, not only on government bonds but also on bank credit. The additional cost of credit, which is a recurrent burden, makes it practically impossible for the heavily indebted countries to regain competitiveness.

This is not the result of an evil plot. It was caused by a lack of understanding of an extremely complicated reality. In my articles, I put forward a series of practical proposals that could have worked at the time but became inadequate soon thereafter. Conversely, had the authorities adopted earlier some measures that they were willing to adopt later, they could have arrested the downtrend and then reversed it by adopting further measures. As it is, they have managed to calm the crisis but have failed to reverse the trend.

This analysis emphasizes the vital role that fallibility plays in shaping the course of history: there would have been no crisis without it. It also shows that in far-from-equilibrium conditions, the normal rules don't apply. One of the reasons the crisis persists is that the eurozone is governed by treaties that were designed for near-equilibrium conditions. Obviously, economists relying on the prevailing paradigm could not have reached this conclusion.

Fat Tails

Both the superbubble and the euro crisis are examples of far-from-equilibrium situations. A core difference between my approach and mainstream economics is that my framework can accommodate and explain such phenomena. Instead of declaring equilibrium as the outcome, I distinguish between near-equilibrium conditions that are characterized by random fluctuations and far-from-equilibrium situations that produce initially self-reinforcing but eventually self-defeating trends. A near-equilibrium situation yields humdrum, everyday events that are repetitive and lend themselves to statistical generalizations. In contrast, far-from-equilibrium conditions give rise to unique, historic events in which outcomes are uncertain but have the capacity to disrupt the statistical generalizations based on everyday events. Rules that can usefully guide decisions in near-equilibrium conditions can be misleading in far-from-equilibrium situations.

The financial crisis of 2007–2008 is a case in point. All the risk management tools and synthetic financial products that were based on the assumption that price deviations from a putative equilibrium occur in a random fashion broke down, and those who relied on mathematical models that had served them well in near-equilibrium conditions got badly hurt.

In the 1960s, the mathematician Benoit Mandelbrot (1963) discovered that the price movements of financial assets sometimes exhibit "fat tails"—more extreme events than a normal Gaussian distribution would predict. This finding has since been confirmed by much research. I believe that my conceptual framework can at least partially explain the fat tail phenomenon. Reality feeds the participants so much information that they need to introduce dichotomies and other simplifying devices to make some sense of it. The simplest way to introduce order is binary division; hence the tendency to use dichotomies. When markets switch from one side of a dichotomy to another, the transition can be quite violent. The tipping point is difficult to predict, but it is associated with a sharp increase in volatility, which manifests itself in fat tails.

Toward a New Paradigm

One of the most powerful concepts for purposes of simplification is the concept of change. In my first philosophical essay (1962), written under the influence of Karl Popper, I used the concept of change to build models of social systems and reflexively connect them to modes of thinking. I linked organic society with the traditional mode of thinking, open society with the critical mode, and closed society with the dogmatic mode.

It can be seen that my conceptual framework extends to a much broader area than the one covered by economic theory. But financial markets provide the best laboratory for studying far-from-equilibrium situations at work because they manifest themselves in fat tails that can be clearly observed in the data. They can be studied in other fields as well, but only in the form of a historical narrative, as I have done in my analysis of the euro crisis, which weaves together politics with financial economics.

Reflexivity has been largely neglected until recently because it connects different fields studied by different disciplines. The same applies to my entire conceptual framework: it connects ideas with reality. Reality has been broken up into narrow fields of specialization. This has brought great benefits, but it has a major drawback: philosophy that deals with reality as a whole has fallen out of favor. It needs to be rehabilitated.

Mainstream economics tried to seal itself off from reality by relying on postulates that turned out to be far removed from reality. The financial crisis of 2007–2008 and subsequent events exposed the weakness of this approach. The bankruptcy of Lehman Brothers was also the bankruptcy of the prevailing paradigm. There is urgent need for a new one.

This essay has shown that my interpretation of financial markets—based on my theory of reflexivity—is radically different from orthodox economics based on efficient markets and rational expectations. Strictly speaking, both interpretations are pseudo-scientific by Popper's standards. That is why I called my first book *The Alchemy of Finance*. And that is why some proponents of the efficient market hypothesis still defend it in the face of all the evidence.

Nevertheless, I contend that my interpretation yields better explanations and predictions than the prevailing paradigm. How can I reconcile this claim with my starting contention that the future is inherently uncertain and financial markets are inherently unpredictable? By resorting to Popper's logic of scientific discovery. As a market participant, I formulate conjectures and expose them to refutation. I also assume that other market participants are doing the same thing, whether they realize it or not. Their expectations are usefully aggregated in market prices. I can therefore compare my own expectations with prevailing prices. When I see a divergence, I see a profit opportunity. The bigger the divergence, the bigger the opportunity. Popper made a similar assertion about scientific hypotheses. Philosophers of science roundly criticized him for this on the grounds that the predictive power of scientific theories cannot be quantified. It may not work for scientific theories, but I can testify from personal experience that it does work in the alchemy of financial markets.

When the price behavior contradicts my expectations I have to reexamine my hypothesis. If I find myself proven wrong, I take a loss; if I conclude that the market is wrong, I increase my bet, always taking into account the risk that I am bound to be wrong some of the time. This works well in markets that are efficient in the sense that transaction costs are minimal; it does not work in private equity investments that are not readily marketable. My performance record bears this out. I was successful in markets, but not in private equities. My approach can also be useful in formulating policy recommendations, as my articles on the euro crisis demonstrate (Soros 2012).

5. CONCLUSION

Ever since the crash of 2008 there has been widespread recognition, both among economists and the general public, that economic theory has failed. But there is no consensus on the causes and the extent of that failure.

I have argued that the failure is more profound than generally recognized. It goes back to the foundations of economic theory. Economics tried to model itself on Newtonian physics. It sought to establish universally and timelessly valid laws governing reality. But economics is a social science, and there is a fundamental difference between the natural and the social sciences. Social phenomena have thinking participants who cannot base their decisions on perfect knowledge, yet they cannot avoid making decisions because avoiding them also counts as a decision. They introduce an element of indeterminacy into the course of human events that is absent in the behavior of inanimate objects. The resulting uncertainty hinders the social sciences in producing laws similar to Newton's physics. Yet once we recognize this difference, it frees us to develop new approaches to the study of social phenomena. Although they have not yet been fully developed, they hold out great promise.

The stakes could not be higher. The mistaken theories that allowed the superbubble to build, the policy errors that were made in the wake of the crash, and the ongoing mishandling of the euro crisis highlight the human suffering that can result from a fundamental misunderstanding of the nature of economic systems. Recognizing the implications of our fallibility will be a great improvement in our understanding.

Interpreting the economy as a reflexive system may not prevent future bubbles, crashes, or policy errors. But it may enable deeper insights into economic and sociopolitical phenomena and help humankind to better manage its affairs in the future.

I realize that my approach is still very rudimentary. For most of my life, I developed it in the privacy of my own mind. Only in recent years did I have the benefit of substantive criticism. It remains to be seen whether my conceptual framework can develop into a new paradigm. Much depends on whether reflexive feedback loops can be properly modeled. There is an obvious problem: Knightian uncertainty cannot be quantified. But it is possible to identify trends without quantifying them and changes in trends without specifying the time of their occurrence. That is what I have done in my boom-bust model (Figure 4). We can also use volatility, which is quantifiable, as a substitute for uncertainty. And there may be other techniques that address these issues, such as imperfect knowledge economics (Frydman and Goldberg 2013) or new approaches yet to be invented.

The new paradigm is bound to be very different from the one that failed. It cannot be timeless; it must recognize that some changes are nonrecurring, whereas others exhibit statistical regularities. Moreover, economic theory will not be able to seal itself off from other disciplines and from reality. It cannot confine itself to studying the allocation of limited means among unlimited alternative ends; it will have to take into account the impact the allocation may have on prevailing values and methods of production.

Obviously, I shall not be able to develop my ideas on my

own. That is why I am so pleased that the *Journal of Economic Methodology* is publishing a special issue on reflexivity.

REFERENCES

Beinhocker, Eric D. 2013. "Reflexivity, Complexity and the Nature of Social Science." *Journal of Economic Methodology* 20 (4).

Frydman, Roman, and Michael D. Goldberg. 2013. "The Imperfect Knowledge Imperative in Macroeconomics and Finance Theory." Chapter 4 in *Rethinking Expectations: The Way Forward for Macroeconomics*, ed. Roman Frydman and Edmund S. Phelps. Princeton: Princeton University Press.

Keynes, John Maynard. 1936. *The General Theory of Employment, Interest, and Money*. New York: Harcourt Brace.

Knight, Frank H. 1921. *Risk, Uncertainty, and Profit*. Boston: Houghton Mifflin.

Mandelbrot, Benoit. 1963. "The Variation of Certain Speculative Prices." *Journal of Business* 36: 394–419.

Merton, Robert K. 1949. *Social Theory and Social Structure*. New York: Free Press.

Popper, Karl. 1935. *Logik der Forschung*. Vienna: Verlag von Julius Springer. First English edition 1959, *The Logic of Scientific Discovery*. London: Hutchinson.

———. 1944. "The Poverty of Historicism, II. A Criticism of Historicist Methods." *Economica* 43 (11): 119–137.

———. 1945. *The Open Society and Its Enemies*. London: Routledge.

———. 1957. *The Poverty of Historicism*. London: Routledge.

Robbins, Lionel. 1932. *An Essay on the Nature and Significance of Economic Science*. London: Macmillan.

Soros, George. 1962. *Burden of Consciousness*. Unpublished; revised version included in Soros (2006).

———. 1987. *The Alchemy of Finance*. Hoboken, NJ: Wiley and Sons.

———. 1998. *The Crisis of Global Capitalism: Open Society Endangered*. New York: PublicAffairs.

———. 2000. *Open Society: Reforming Global Capitalism*. New York: PublicAffairs.

———. 2006. *The Age of Fallibility: Consequences of the War on Terror*. New York: PublicAffairs.

———. 2008. *The New Paradigm for Financial Markets: The Credit Crisis and What It Means*. New York: PublicAffairs.

———. 2009. *The Crash of 2008 and What It Means: The New Paradigm for Financial Markets*. New York: PublicAffairs.

———. 2010. *The Soros Lectures at the Central European University*. New York: PublicAffairs.

———. 2012. *Financial Turmoil in the United States and Europe: Essays*. New York: PublicAffairs.

GEORGE SOROS is chairman of Soros Fund Management and is the founder of a global network of foundations dedicated to supporting open societies. He is the author of several bestselling books including *The Crash of 2008: The New Paradigm for Financial Markets*; *The Crisis of Global Capitalism*; *The Bubble of American Supremacy*; *Underwriting Democracy*; and *The Age of Fallibility*. He was born in Budapest and lives in New York City.

DR. GREGOR PETER SCHMITZ is currently Europe correspondent of *Der Spiegel*. From 2007 to 2013 he served as Washington correspondent. Prior to his award-winning journalistic work, Schmitz was director of the Brussels office of an international think tank. Schmitz holds a law degree from Munich University and is a graduate of Sciences–Po, Paris. He also earned graduate degrees from Cambridge University and Harvard University.

PublicAffairs is a publishing house founded in 1997. It is a tribute to the standards, values, and flair of three persons who have served as mentors to countless reporters, writers, editors, and book people of all kinds, including me.

I. F. Stone, proprietor of *I. F. Stone's Weekly*, combined a commitment to the First Amendment with entrepreneurial zeal and reporting skill and became one of the great independent journalists in American history. At the age of eighty, Izzy published *The Trial of Socrates*, which was a national bestseller. He wrote the book after he taught himself ancient Greek.

Benjamin C. Bradlee was for nearly thirty years the charismatic editorial leader of *The Washington Post*. It was Ben who gave the *Post* the range and courage to pursue such historic issues as Watergate. He supported his reporters with a tenacity that made them fearless and it is no accident that so many became authors of influential, best-selling books.

Robert L. Bernstein, the chief executive of Random House for more than a quarter century, guided one of the nation's premier publishing houses. Bob was personally responsible for many books of political dissent and argument that challenged tyranny around the globe. He is also the founder and longtime chair of Human Rights Watch, one of the most respected human rights organizations in the world.

• • •

For fifty years, the banner of Public Affairs Press was carried by its owner Morris B. Schnapper, who published Gandhi, Nasser, Toynbee, Truman, and about 1,500 other authors. In 1983, Schnapper was described by *The Washington Post* as "a redoubtable gadfly." His legacy will endure in the books to come.

Peter Osnos, *Founder and Editor-at-Large*